D1235241

Handbook on the Psychology of Pricing

100+ EFFECTS ON PERSUASION AND
INFLUENCE EVERY ENTREPRENEUR,
MARKETER AND PRICING MANAGER
NEEDS TO KNOW

Dr. Markus Husemann-Kopetzky

Pricing School Press

Copyright © 2018 by Markus Husemann-Kopetzky.

All rights reserved. No part of this publication may be reproduced, distributed, or transmitted in any form or by any means, including photocopying, recording, or other electronic or mechanical methods, without the prior written permission of the author, except in the case of brief quotations embodied in critical reviews and certain other non-commercial uses permitted by copyright law.

Handbook on the Psychology of Pricing – first edition
by Markus Husemann-Kopetzky
ISBN 978-3-947897-00-1

For free book updates visit us at

www.PsychologyOfPricing.com

TESTIMONIALS

"Dr. Markus Husemann-Kopetzky has written a book that will be of immense, practical help to everyone involved in selling or price setting. The *Handbook on the Psychology of Pricing* clearly presents over one-hundred psychological pricing effects backed by solid research. This book is an absolute must-read for any business owner or marketer."

BRIAN TRACY
BEST-SELLING AUTHOR
"THE PSYCHOLOGY OF SELLING"

"The author packed decades of research into a readable, comprehensive manual on pricing psychology. This book is an absolute must-read for every manager interested in exciting customers, driving growth, and increasing profits."

CHRISTIAN GASPLMAYR
DIRECTOR SALES AND CONSUMER
INTERACTION TRANSFORMATION
SWAROVSKI

"This book is packed with intriguing, powerful insights that will expand your perspective on pricing. A must-read for all managers who have to make profitable pricing decisions."

DR. ANDRÉ HINTSCHES
HEAD OF INTERNATIONAL PRICING, USED CARS
VOLKSWAGEN FINANCIAL SERVICES

"The *Handbook on the Psychology of Pricing* is at its best in consolidating 'the art' of psychological pricing. It offers a wealth of insights that can inspire every company – big and small, high-tech and low-tech. This book is an absolute must-have on every marketer's bookshelf!"

SIMONE MOSER
MARKETING MANAGER
BSH HOME APPLIANCES

"If you ever wondered what psychological levers pricing managers have at their hands, you will find it in the *Handbook on Psychology of Pricing*. This is the most comprehensive coverage on the topic available. An indispensable resource for all pricing managers."

MARTIN JARMATZ, PHD
STRATEGIC PRICING MANAGER
TDC GROUP

"To the point. No fluff. No insights wrapped in lengthy story telling. The *Handbook on the Psychology of Pricing* is a rich source of inspiration and a must read for any entrepreneur."

SIMON KRÄMER
ENTREPRENEUR
FLOWERART

"Outstanding. Every time I open the *Handbook on the Psychology of Pricing*, I find new ideas for my company and my clients' businesses to drive growth and profitability."

MARTIN FYRST
FOUNDER
TRACTION BUSINESS

"The *Handbook on the Psychology of Pricing* breaks new ground in the breadth and depth on psychological pricing. This book is a must-read for anyone who want to realize the powerful forces psychological pricing has on a company's financial performance of any size."

LOA FRIDFINNSON
CHIEF CREATIVE STRATEGIST
ACTIV8 | CORPORATE RELATIONS

"The author does a brilliant job in distilling the practical core of academic research. The *Handbook on the Psychology of Pricing* offers a new perspective on how pricing innovations impact customer behavior and grow business. The insights in this book are priceless."

PROF. DR. MIKE HOFFMEISTER
FOUNDER OF THE INTERNATIONAL TREND FORUM
MARKETING PROFESSOR
OSTFALIA UNIVERSITY OF APPLIED SCIENCES

Contents

To Sabine, Sophia and Luisa

Reality is merely an illusion, albeit a very persistent one.

—ALBERT EINSTEIN

To Busy Marketers

When I began sketching this book three years ago, I sought to write for you – a business owner, marketing manager, pricing expert or business student with a time-constrained schedule and a vivid interest in the value psychological pricing can add to the business you are working in and your personal skill profile in particular.

As an academic researcher passionate about the field of psychological pricing, I have read literally hundreds of studies comprised of thousands of pages that unearth findings and recommendations, which could be summarized in a few sentences. This book aims at providing these summaries, the managerially relevant nuggets. To ensure that recommendations and insights are based on solid, replicable research methods, this book solely refers to academic sources. You do not find any anecdotal business wisdom, case studies, war stories or trade secrets in this book. Most importantly, I want to point out that this book is written as part of my academic endeavor and is 100% independent from my current corporate position at Amazon.

Academic pricing research has generated a plethora of insights but buried the lead for professionals. This book assumes a business perspective when analyzing academic papers and tries to give a most concise answer to your imaginative question I always kept in mind: "Interesting study, but so what?"

This book distills 100+ insights and effects on psychological pricing from hundreds of research papers and translates respective findings into actionable recommendations.

The following book is structured in four parts. The first chapter highlights the importance of pricing in general and the contribution of psychological pricing in particular. It proceeds with introducing a framework that provides structure and guidance from a business angle. Chapters two to four are devoted to separate sets of pricing parameters that marketing managers can adjust to optimize prices from a psychological point of view.

Within the latter three chapters, psychological pricing effects are grouped under common themes. For each effect, an overview on the research projects that unearthed a particular effect provides relevant background information, and a short summary distills its key takeaway.

Research on psychological pricing is continuously evolving. New studies and insights are published virtually every month or quarter. To help you stay up to date, I grant you exclusive access to bi-annual updates on psychological pricing research. You are cordially invited to check out your free updates here:

Link: *www.PsychologyOfPricing.com/readersarea*
Password: freeforreaders

As research is evolving so should this book be. Please share your comments, feedback, or your review of this book with me. Also, if you notice important effects that appear to be missed or if you have ideas on research projects that might uncover interesting effects, please let me know at

Markus@PsychologyOfPricing.com

I hope you enjoy this book and take away valuable ideas and inspiration on how to approach pricing through psychological lenses.

CHAPTER 1

Introduction

Pricing Matters

Pricing is the most important arrow marketers hold in their quivers. Among all marketing decisions, pricing exerts a strong influence on customers, directly impacts revenue and profit, and, hence, is critical to business success (Nagle, Hogan, and Zale 2014, p. 15; Winer 2005, p. 3).

To remind ourselves of the four profit drivers managers have at hand: Profit is the difference between revenue and costs. Revenue is the product of *price* and *sold units*. Costs consists of *fixed costs* and *variable costs*, where the latter is the product of *unit cost* and *sold units*. A numerical example borrowed from Hermann Simon (2015), the grand seigneur of pricing consulting, gives an answer to the question on which of the four profit levers managers should focus their attention. Assuming Acme Company builds a product that costs $60 to make and sells it for $100. Currently, it is selling one million units per year. Each year fixed costs incur of $30 million. Hence, total revenues are $100 million, total costs sum up to $90 million leaving $10 million in profit.

Now, you are charged with the task of improving profit. On which profit lever should you give highest priority – variable costs, fixed costs, sales volume, or price? A way to answer this question is to look on the individual impact of improving each profit driver by 5%, leaving all other levers untouched.

A cost-cutting project aiming at decreasing fixed costs or variable costs by 5% increases profits by 15% or 30%, respectively. In comparison, pushing volume in a sales optimization project by 5% improves profits by 20%. Finally, a price increase by 5% generates the largest uplift among all profit levers – 50% in additional profit. Table 1 summarizes this example.

Profit driver	Current value	5% improvement	Impact on profit
Price	$100	$105	+$5 Mio. / +50%
Unit sales	1 Mio.	1.05 Mio.	+$2 Mio. / +20%
Variable costs	$60	$57	+$3 Mio. / +30%
Fixed costs	$30 Mio.	$28.5 Mio.	+$1.5 Mio. / +15%
Profit	$10 Mio.		

Table 1: Illustrative example, impact of improving various profit levers

This example shows that price has a strong leverage on profit and profitability – but is it representative for the majority of the business world?

In an often-cited study, Marn and Rosiello (1992) from McKinsey analyzed 2,463 companies and calculated an increase in profit assuming a 1% improvement in each of the four profit drivers. Here is what they found: 1% improvement to fixed cost or variable costs increases profits by 2.3% or 7.8%, respectively. Raising sales volume by 1% raises profits by 3.3%. However, the largest leverage effect has a price increase of 1%: it boosts profits by 11.1%.

Table 2 summarizes findings from an updated version of this classic study covering the 1,200 largest global companies (Baker, Marn, and Zawada 2010) and also looks at the results from a different angle: How much does a profit lever need to improve to double profits?

Profit driver	Impact on profit of 1% improvement	Improvement required to double profit
Price	11.0%	9.1%
Unit sales	3.7%	27.1%
Variable costs	7.2%	13.7%
Fixed costs	2.7%	37.1%

Table 2: Market data, impact of improving various profit levers
(Kohli and Suri 2011)

Knowing that pricing is an effective lever to increase profitability is the first step toward success. The second step is to develop pricing skills to actually put theory into practice. Liozu and Hinterhuber (2013) surveyed 1,800+ pricing professionals, marketers, sales experts, and top managers on their company's pricing capabilities and financial performance. The researchers confirmed that pricing competency directly impacts firms' overall top line and bottom line performance.

This book is written to serve as a stepping-stone to inspire your pricing practice and to further strengthen your pricing skills in the space of psychological pricing.

Psychological Pricing Matters

Pricing determines a company's profitability. Thus, understanding how customers react toward different prices becomes crucial.

Two theories aim at explaining consumer behavior in light of prices: economics and psychology. In the late 19th century, the economist Alfred Marshall (1890) developed a theory of a solely rationally deciding individual who evaluates the value – what an economist calls "utility" – a purchase delivers relative to the amount of wealth he needs to sacrifice. Ideally, this rationalist would allocate his resources across purchases – i.e. pay prices – so that total utility maximizes. This perspective would become known as neoclassical theory.

Neoclassical theory holds some strong assumptions that actual consumer behavior contradicts. For example, one study explicitly compares how economics and marketing researchers treat "pricing" differently (Skouras, Avlonitis, and Indounas 2005). To illustrate this point, we focus on one core assumption: customers receive less value from a purchase with increasing prices, so demand steadily decreases with higher prices and increases with lower prices. In reality, consumer behavior refutes this straightforward relationship – and psychology explains why.

Lower is not always better: Researchers found that consumers associate low prices with low-quality so that consumers do not buy a product if its price drops below a price which indicates a minimum acceptable quality (Monroe 1971a; Stoetzel, Sauerwein, and de Vulpian 1954).

Higher is not always worse: Conversely, at higher prices consumers conclude that products are of better quality so that purchase likelihood increases (Scitovszky 1944). In other cases, people buy products not despite but because they are priced at higher price levels to signal status and wealth to their social peers – an effect known as prestige effect or Veblen effect (Veblen 1899, p. 36): "In order to gain and to hold the esteem of men, it is not sufficient merely to possess wealth or power. The wealth or power must be put in evidence, for esteem is awarded only on evidence."

Price changes do not always matter: Monroe (1973) found that consumers require price changes to pass a perceptual threshold to be recognized as such. This "just noticeable difference" leads to ranges of prices being perceived as identical so that customer purchase behavior does not change with higher prices.

Economics assumes a demand curve with a monotonous downward slope. Psychological pricing research suggests that the shape of a demand curve can (i) follow the shape of a rectangular triangle ("minimum price effect"), (ii) resemble a turned-over U ("price quality inference") and/or (iii) remain parallel to the price axis ("price indifference"). Figure 1 depicts differences in demand curves between neoclassical theory and findings in psychological pricing research.

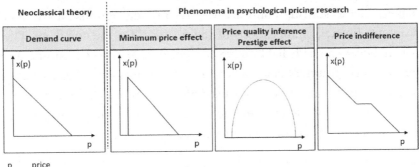

p   price
x(p)   demand in units as function of price

Figure 1: Demand curve in neoclassical theory vs.
psychological pricing research

To summarize, these three examples demonstrate that psychological or behavioral pricing research predicts and explains consumer behavior better than traditional economics at least under specific circumstances.

In the following, we discuss more than 100 such behavioral pricing effects that neoclassical theory defines as anomalies.

4-P Model of Psychological Pricing Management

The purpose of this book is to help decision-makers apply a wide variety of pricing research findings to concrete pricing decisions. Many discussions with fellow researchers and pricing managers revealed that a framework adds value here. A few organizing schemes have been proposed in pricing research. These schemes either structure research findings according to different stages during which customers process price information (e.g. price information acquisition, price evaluation, price storage, spending and consumption behavior; see Koschate-Fischer and Wüllner 2017) or cluster past studies more or less arbitrarily by a common theme (e.g. "reference price" or "price fairness"; see Somervuori 2014).

This book is written for managers dealing with pricing decisions. Consequently, the following model starts and ends with the decision-maker. At the starting point are various pricing options; at the end point are financial implications of the decision for the company. The part in between sheds light on psychological processes explaining differences in consumer behavior. The 4-P model of psychological pricing management breaks down the causal chain from pricing options to financial impact into four components each building upon the preceding: parameters, processes, phenomena, and profits.

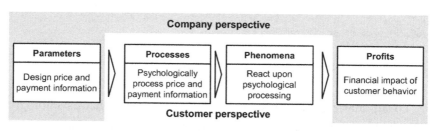

Figure 2: 4-P model of psychological pricing management

Parameters summarize all levers that marketers and pricing experts can pull to design price and payment information. The following chapters differentiate these price parameters into price design parameters, price context parameters and price payment parameters. Price design parameters refer to the focal price of a specific offering (e.g. odd price effect). Price context parameters consider all other factors that impact customers' price perception beyond the focal price (e.g. decoy effect). And, finally, price payment parameters design the actual money transfer from the customer to the company, which influences how the former perceives prices in the first place (e.g. credit card effect).

Processes explain how consumers process and evaluate price and payment information as designed by parameters in step 1.

Phenomena describe and predict consumers' reactions and behaviors as a result of their psychological processing.

Profits quantify customer behavior that was initially triggered by price parameters and driven by psychological processing.

The present book focusses on academic research that shows how consumers react to different price and payment information and explains the theoretical underpinnings of the respective customer behavior. Hence, this book stresses the first three p's: parameters, processes and phenomena. As we will usually cover all three p's in conjunction when we discuss a specific price parameter, their differentiation may not seem to be useful. However, mentally separating these categories is valuable as it structures our thinking when considering changes to prices.

Guiding questions are always: What can we change in terms of prices, contextual information, and payment process? How will customers perceive this information? How will customers react upon their perception?

Two other important questions need to be left to another book placing more emphasis on research methods, experimental designs, and financial modelling: How to (statistically) relate changes in actual customer behavior to differently designed price parameters? How to quantify the financial impact of changes in customer behavior due to changes in price parameters?

One word on the way effects are categorized and labelled: As you will see in the following sections, assigning a specific effect to just a single category is sometimes rather a matter of taste than a clear-cut decision. Pricing is as much art as it is science.

CHAPTER 2

Price Design Parameters

Price design parameters are at the core of a pricing decision. Studies summarized in this chapter reveal how consumers respond to subtle changes in the number of a price or its presentation. These effects reveal different options that you use to set a price.

Grouped into eight categories, we will cover 65 effects on how to design a focal price

1. *Number Design* shows how consumers recognize and perceive numerical values of prices.

2. *Phonetic Design* reveals the impact of differences in pronounced number words on price perception.

3. *Visual Design* demonstrates how individuals react differently to visual cues of the same numerical price.

4. *Sale Prices and Discounts* summarizes studies that guide pricing decisions when presenting the current price as a sale price.

5. *Partitioned Pricing* provides an overview on studies of how to best present prices when the total price of one product consists of various components (e.g. product price plus shipping and handling fees).

6. *Price Bundling* summarizes strategies on presenting prices for multiple products bundled together (e.g. PC plus printer or multipacks of the same product).

7. *Price Changes* sheds light on how consumers perceive adjustments to prices.

8. *Price Level & Price Mechanisms* summarizes how consumers react to higher price levels and specific pricing methods (flat rate tariffs or trade-in pricing).

Number Design

Odd Price Effect

Price endings in nine are among the most well-known and longest researched effects in psychological pricing. But do odd prices – i.e. prices just below even figures, e. g. $1.99 instead of $2 or $299 instead of $300 – drive demand in comparison to their round counterparts?

In an early report, Ginzberg (1936) briefly described an experiment in which a catalog retailer mailed catalogs with round prices and "just under" prices. Results from this experiment were mixed; demand increased for a few products and remained the same or dropped for others. Some later studies also delivered inconsistent results. However, Schindler and Kibarian (1996) attributed these to inadequate methods applied in the research conducted.

To overcome methodological issues, these researchers ran an experiment in cooperation with a direct-mail women's clothing retailer. They distributed three versions of an otherwise identical catalog to three customer segments of 30,000 each. In the catalog, they set prices either at a round amount (e.g. $23), one cent below (e.g. $22.99), or 12 cents below (e.g. $22.88). The last option was included as it reflected the past practice of the retailer. Schindler and Kibarian (1996) found that all three versions would make roughly the same number of customers buy (no statistical difference) but lead to higher per-capita spending for 88 and 99 endings compared to 00 endings with 99 endings being more effective.

Anderson and Simester (2003) collaborated with a mail-order retailer and distributed catalogs with different price versions to more than 140,000 customers. The researchers found, first, that prices ending in nine increase demand, second, that this effect is stronger for new compared to established products and, third, that this effect is reduced when an "on sale" claim was attached to the respective product.

The reasons why consumers react to price endings appear to be threefold.

First, a level effect occurs when consumers process price figures from left to right placing more weight on the left most digits. Stiving and Winer (1997) showed that participants in an experiment prefer a sale price of $0.79 compared to a regular price of $0.93 much more than a sale price of $0.75 next to a regular price of $0.89 although the absolute discount was the same and the relative discount in the latter case was actually larger. Processing numbers from left to right explains this effect: in the first sale price example, the difference between the left-most price digits is two (9–7); in the second example, it's just one (8–7). More details on the cognitive explanation of odd prices are given in the section on the left digit effect.

Second, an image effect suggests that consumers infer a special meaning from prices ending in nine. As retailers use odd prices more often than even when promoting sales and discounts, consumers have "learned" to associate odd prices with discounts (Schindler 2006). Therefore, odd prices carry a connotation of low prices for consumers and convey messages like "cannot find this item at a lower price," "the item is on sale," or "price has not been recently raised," among other inferences people make (Schindler 1991; Schindler and Kibarian 2001).

Third, a perceived-gain effect results when consumers take a round price as the reference price and consider the difference to the odd-price as a gain. As the value function – according to prospect theory – is relatively steep for small gains (due to convex shape) these small gains receive a disproportionately high value despite their little monetary value (Schindler and Kirby 1997).

What are potential caveats with odd pricing? For retailers whose products are of high quality, "99" price endings could potentially hurt consumers' perception of product quality (Schindler and Kibarian 2001).

Use odd prices by default but consider implications on quality perceptions.

Odd Price Effect Refined: 95 vs. 99

You are about to buy a fly spray. Does it matter whether it is priced at $3.95 or $3.99?

Gendall, Fox, and Wilton (1998) ran an experiment with fast-moving consumer goods (fly spray, cheese) and durables (electric kettles). They found that prices with endings in 99 cents are more attractive for low-priced, fast-moving consumer goods (FMCG) than 95 endings, whereas prices that end in 95 cents have a stronger impact on demand for higher priced products (in this experiment, $50) than endings in 99 cents. These results are particularly interesting for low-priced items as consumers actually prefer slightly higher prices.

The effectiveness of odd-price endings depends on price level. For low-priced products, it's better to use 99; for high-priced products, let prices end in 95.

Left Digit Effect: Why Do Odd Price Endings Work

Imagine you need to buy shampoo. Two of your favorite brands are on sale: brand A: $2.99 instead of $4, brand B: $3.10 instead of $4.10. Which deal is more appealing?

When comparing a price that ends with a nine to a round price, consumers evaluate the odd price differently only if the first – the left – digit also changes (Thomas and Morwitz 2005), i.e. $2.99 vs. $3, but not $2.79 vs. $2.80.

Numerical cognition explains this process. People tend to evaluate multi-digit numbers holistically by mapping them on a mental line (Restle 1970). As we read Arabic numbers from left to right, consumers might be anchored at the first digit. This anchoring causes respondents to perceive the distance on their mental line between two prices starting with different digits (two vs. three) to be larger than between two prices of the same first digit despite sharing the same mathematical difference of one cent (Thomas and Morwitz 2005).

To test this "left digit effect," Thomas and Morwitz (2005) showed participants pairs of ads for pens. They kept the price for one pen fixed at $4 (standard price) and changed the price for the other pen (target price). Then participants were asked to rate their magnitude perception on a five-point scale. The researchers found that participants evaluate a target price of $2.99 as significantly lower than a price of $3 whereas they do not rate a price of $2.79 vs. $2.80 or $3.19 vs. $3.20 being any different.

What are boundary conditions of this effect? With increasing distance between two numbers, people can more easily differentiate the magnitude of two numbers being compared (Moyer and Landauer 1967) – an effect called distance effect, which was repeatedly confirmed for prices as well (Xia 2003). This distance effect causes the left-digit effect to diminish as both numbers become easier to discriminate (Thomas and Morwitz 2005). In another experiment, the researchers set the standard price $1 and $2 higher and lower than the target price and chose target prices of $3.99 or $4. When the difference between the standard and target price was $1, participants perceived the target prices that end in nine ($5 vs. $3.99) as significantly lower than its round version ($5 vs. $4). However, when the distance increased to $2 people rated differences in the odd price condition ($6 vs. $3.99) and the round price condition ($6 vs. $4) as the same.

Lin and Wang (2017) followed up on these findings and looked at the impact of number of digits on the left-digit effect. They found that for low three-digit prices (e.g. NT$200 vs. NT$199) the left-digit effect was stronger than for high three-digit price (e.g. NT$800 vs. NT$799) but diminished for four-digit prices (e.g. NT$2,000 vs. NT$1,999).

When comparing two prices, consumers evaluate a price that ends with a nine as significantly lower than a slightly higher round price only if the left digit changes. This effect diminishes with increasing distance between regular price and sales price and for high-priced products (high three-digit prices and four-digit prices).

Rounded Price Effect

When buying perfume as a gift for a friend, which price feels better: $39.72 or $40? Does a better feeling for a price translate into higher purchase likelihood?

Consumers feel when the price is right. Wadhwa and Zhang (2015) found that round prices feel more right for hedonic, emotion-based products, whereas odd prices are appropriate for utilitarian, cognition-based products. The research coined this finding the "rounded price effect." In an experiment, the research team asked participants to indicate their purchase likelihood for two products: As a hedonic product, the researchers chose a bottle of champagne to be bought as a gift for a friend, and as utilitarian product, they decided for a calculator with a detailed description of all functionalities. The prices were manipulated at three levels: rounded ($40), non-rounded/low ($39.72) and non-rounded/high ($40.28). The experiment revealed that customers indicated a higher likelihood to buy a hedonic product at a round price than at any non-rounded price. The opposite is true for utilitarian products: Customers would prefer non-rounded prices to rounded prices. The differences between high and low non-rounded prices were insignificant for both products.

Whether a product is considered as hedonic or utilitarian depends on the consumption goal (Dhar and Wertenbroch 2000). A camera could be a utilitarian product if bought for a class project but considered a hedonic product when purchased for a family vacation. The research team tested this scenario in an experiment and presented participants with the same description of the camera but told either half of the group that it bought this camera for a class project or a family vacation. As part of the experiment, the researcher handed out sample photos the camera presumably took and asked participants to evaluate the quality of the pictures and to rank their anticipated satisfaction with the purchase. When the camera carried an odd price ($101.53) the utilitarian group rated the quality of the pictures as well as their anticipated satisfaction as higher compared to those who were exposed to a rounded price ($100). The opposite turned out to be true for the hedonic group. The camera at the rounded price received better quality and satisfaction ratings than at the unrounded price.

Get to know why customers buy your products and whether their decision is triggered by emotions or cognitions. Use round prices for hedonic products and non-round prices for utilitarian products.

Right Digit Effect

When deciding about digits on the right-hand side of a price, psychological effects go beyond odd versus even pricing.

In the field of numerical cognitions, researchers found that people can more easily differentiate smaller numbers (less than five) than larger numbers (larger than five) – an effect called magnitude effect (Dehaene, Dupoux, and Mehler 1990).

Coulter and Coulter (2007) applied this finding to prices and let participants in an experiment evaluate perceived discounts and purchase likelihood for different pairs of regular and sale prices. Consumers were more likely to buy when prices ended in small right digits (regular price: $244, sale price: $233) and reported higher perceived savings than for prices ending in higher right digits ($199 vs. $188) although the relative discount for the latter pair was objectively higher.

Choose regular and sale prices so that the sale price's right digit is below the regular price's and that both right digits are smaller than five.

Price Precision Effect

Assume you are about to buy a house. The price is $484,880. What would be your counter offer? Would your counter offer change if the price was $485,000?

When communicating about small magnitudes we usually use precise numbers, whereas when we make statements about large magnitudes, large, round numbers are more common (Dehaene and Mehler

1992). Thomas, Simon, and Kadiyali (2010) argue that precise, large numbers cause uncertainty on the side of consumers because they expect a more round number. This uncertainty makes consumers pay attention to the relationship between precision and magnitude. As we learned from past experience that precise numbers are used for small prices, consumers perceive a precise, large price as smaller than a rounded, actually lower, price. This effect of associating a smaller magnitude with more precise prices is coined price precision effect.

In an experiment Thomas, Simon, and Kadiyali (2010) asked participants to judge whether a price was high or low on an 11-point scale. In the context of house prices, the researches selected six price pairs consisting of a round price and a slightly higher, precise price – for example $390,000 and $391,534. The relative price difference ranged from 0.08% to 0.39%. The group of participants was split and each half was asked to rate a different set of six standalone prices with each price being picked from one price pair. In this way, no participants saw both prices of the same price pair. The experiment confirmed that participants gave the higher, precise prices a lower magnitude rating than round prices.

Moving from the lab to the real world, the research team turned to the real estate market and developed the hypothesis that houses with more precise list prices would result in higher actually paid sale prices. The research team analyzed more than 16,000 house sales in two real estate markets and found that the more precise the list price – i.e. prices with fewer than three ending zeroes – indeed led to higher sale prices. Estimating the size of this effect, the statistical model suggested that customers' additional willingness to pay for a house at a precise list price (e.g. $484,880) compared to a similar round list price (e.g. $485,000) is about $1,300.

In the context of six-digit prices, customers perceive prices that are more precise as lower than slightly lower round prices.

Symmetric Price Effect

Would you describe yourself as someone with a sense for aesthetics? Moreover, could you imagine this sense would affect your perception of prices?

People have an inclination for symmetry due to aesthetic reasons. Dobson, Gorman, and Moore (2010) found support that this preference also extends to prices.

In an experiment, the researchers showed that participants preferred a vertically mirrored price ($810,018) over a slightly lower price ($805,099).

In the context of six-digit prices customers prefer vertically mirrored, symmetrical prices.

Implicit Egotism: When Numbers Carry a Meaning

We learned from social psychology that people have a strong tendency to think positively about themselves (e.g. Pelham, Carvallo, and Jones 2005). If somebody or something reminds people of themselves, these positive associations spill over to the reminding subject or object. Pelham, Mirenberg, and Jones (2002) termed this process "implicit egotism." Implicit egotism explains why people have a stronger tendency to marry people sharing the same birthday numbers (Jones et al. 2004), why people move to cities resembling their name (Pelham, Mirenberg, and Jones 2002) or why people are more likely to bet on numbers in lotteries that are part of their birthday (Wang et al. 2016). These examples already suggest two trigger points causing subconscious implicit egotism that we look at: birthday numbers and sports team numbers [see following section], and name letters [see section in "Phonetic Design Parameters"].

People view prices that remind them of themselves more positively.

Birthday Number Effect

Implicit egotism explains that people like their birthday numbers more as these numbers subconsciously remind people of themselves.

Coulter and Grewal (2014) ran an experiment in which consumers saw a pasta dinner promotion for a restaurant. The price was set at $39 but the cents would either match or not match the participant's birthday.

When consumers were exposed to their birthday number in the price, they stated a higher purchase intention than those in the no match condition.

Consumers prefer prices that contain their birthday number over prices with any unrelated number.

Sports Team Number Effect

Are you a football fan – maybe you cheer for San Francisco? Then you already know the number representing this sports team: 49.

Husemann-Kopetzky and Köcher (2017) extended the birthday number price to not only positively but also negatively valenced associations. Two German soccer teams rank among the top 20 rivalries in the soccer world (The Telegraph 2017): Schalke 04 (common abbreviation for "Fussballclub Gelsenkirchen-Schalke 04 e. V.") and BVB 09 (common abbreviation for "Ballspielverein Borussia 09 e. V. Dortmund"). The researchers hypothesized that a fan who, for example, supports BVB 09 would strongly prefer a price ending in decimals 09 over a lower price, but strongly dislikes a price ending of 04 compared with a higher price. The researchers confirmed this effect in an experiment conducted within a soccer context involving fans from both teams as participants. However, in an additional experiment, the researchers invited participants from each team's hometown without a soccer context. The researchers showed participants pairs of restaurant offers and asked participants which they would choose (also known as "choice-based conjoint analysis"). After the participants rated these offers, the researchers asked them whether they were soccer fans and which team they supported. The results were similar to the first experiment: BVB 09 fans would pay a higher price for offers ending in 09 and a (much) lower price for prices ending in 04. For Schalke 09 fans the results were reversed.

Finally, Husemann-Kopetzky and Köcher conducted an experiment involving real purchases. The researchers set up a booth at an open house event at TU Dortmund University (the university located in BVB 09's hometown) to sell waffles with two different toppings – powdered sugar and cinnamon sugar. The prices were set at two different levels (€1.04 and €1.09) and switched every 30 minutes. After each purchase, the researchers asked customers to indicate whether they were soccer fans and which team they supported. About 50% of customers favored BVB 09. The researchers found that a price change (actually price increase) from €1.04 to €1.09 for cinnamon sugar waffles doubled the share of BVB 09 customers choosing this topping from 22.2% to 44.4% while leaving the respective share unchanged for non-soccer fans.

This research demonstrates that consumers hold positive and negative associations with specific objects. Activating these associations directly affects customer behavior and purchase decisions on an unconscious level.

Consumers express a strong preference for or against a price, product etc. when marketing (unconsciously) reminds them of positively or negatively charged associations.

Superstitious Prices

In Western and Eastern cultures, different numbers carry connotations of good or bad luck. In western cultures, "13" is considered unlucky, whereas in eastern cultures, "8" resembles luck, but "4" stands for bad luck. The origins of the former are less clear: the number 13 might trace back to the biblical reference of the 13th guest at the Last Supper who betrayed Jesus (Westjohn, Roschk, and Magnusson 2017).

On the other hand, in Chinese the numbers eight and four are phonetically similar to the words for "luck" and "death." Hence, Simmons and Schindler (2003) found that eight is overrepresented and four underrepresented in Chinese advertisements. In western countries, pricing tactics usually refer to odd pricing (9) versus even pricing (0) instead of price endings carrying specific meanings based on cultural beliefs.

This is interesting as the U.K.-based newspaper *The Guardian* conducted a poll recently asking people their favorite number. After 44,000 responses, the survey announced number 7 as the winner (*The Guardian* 2014). Although scientific research has not looked into the attractiveness of price endings in seven, a few practitioners – in particular in the digital products industry (e.g. online courses) – adopt prices endings in seven.

Nevertheless, are prices that end in lucky eights indeed more attractive to eastern customers or is this tactic a mere business myth? Westjohn, Roschk, and Magnusson (2017) found in various experiments that Singaporean consumers evaluate eight-ending prices as more appealing, in particular when consumers were highly involved in the purchase decision.

As an interesting side note, this superstition effect explains why Chinese bidders in an auction for car license plates in Hong Kong bid on average 63.5% higher prices for each additional "8" on a four-digit plate, and placed 11% lower bids for each "4" (Ng, Chong, and Du 2010).

For Asian customers set prices with endings in eights and avoid fours.

Price of Zero Effect

Does it matter if you charge one cent or nothing for your product?

Shampanier, Mazar, and Ariely (2007) tested this question in a couple of experiments. In one experiment, the researchers offered customers in a cafeteria a piece of chocolate at the checkout. Two kinds of chocolates were offered: Hershey's for 1 cent and Lindt for 14 cents. At these prices, 8% decided for Hershey's, 30% for Lindt, the rest (62%) for no chocolate. Then the researchers reduced the price for each chocolate by one cent, thus, giving Hershey's away for free and charging 13 cents for Lindt. The demand for Hershey's almost quadrupled to 31%, Lindt dropped to 13%, and 56% did not take any chocolate.

What causes the attractiveness of this new pricing? The answer: emotion. When participants in another experiment were asked to indicate their happiness (on a 1 to 5 scale), subjects gave substantially higher ratings when the price for Hershey's was zero (avg. 4.10) compared to when it was one cent (avg. 2.82).

However, the researchers also found that the zero-price effect diminishes when participants were forced to cognitively analyze the offerings at hand and take the time to look more deeply at the products being offered.

When offering a promotion for low price items you should consider whether to give them away for free.

Related Numbers Effect

What is your spontaneous reaction to following discount messages? Which one do you intuitively like more?

- Regular price $100, sale price $30, discount 70%, you save $70
- Regular price $99, sale price $33, discount 66%, you save $66
- Regular price $101, sale price $29, discount 71%, you save $72

Coulter and Roggeveen (2014) reasoned that consumers more fluently process – and therefore like – discount messages more if the presented numbers are related to one other. They either belong to the same approximation sequence (10, 20, 30, 40, ...) or are number multiples (3 x 3 = 9). The researchers conducted an experiment, randomly assigned subjects to one of the three introductory discount messages, recorded their response time, and solicited their deal liking and purchase intentions.

Results showed that subjects took significantly less time to process either of the first two discount frames and expressed higher ratings for deal liking and purchase intentions – although the third option was economically more attractive.

In summary, related numbers in discount messages improve processing fluency of deals, which, in turn, consumers like more and are more inclined to buy.

Consumers are more willing to buy deals when numbers are related in their discount messages (e.g. regular price, sale price, and discount).

Ease of Computation Effect

If a consumer calculates a discount or determines a price difference in general with more ease compared to less would she rather over- or underestimate this price difference?

Research in numerical cognition demonstrates that people require less time and computational effort to determine which number is the larger if the actual difference is large compared to small – an effect termed distance effect (Dehaene 1989).

Thomas and Morwitz (2009) argue that consumers developed naïve theories in which they wrongly infer that if large differences are relatively easily processed, therefore a quicker processing rate would naturally mean that the difference between numbers involved is large.

People falsely attribute ease-of-computation with larger differences.

The easier consumers compute price differences the larger they perceive a difference between the numbers involved in the computation.

Fluent Price Difference Effect

You decide today is your day and you deserve a treat. You enter a supermarket to buy some sweets and fortunately observe that both your favorite brands are on sale. One is at $1 instead of $3 the other at

$0.99 instead of $1.99. Which of both feels cheaper and justifies indulging in sweets?

Thomas and Morwitz (2009) found that consumers evaluate a distance between numbers as larger when it is easier to compute.

In an experiment, participants were presented with 24 products on sale, and saw the regular and discounted price for each in turn. The experiment covered four price levels (roughly between $1 and $9), two magnitude differences (ca. $1 and $3) and three ease-of-computation conditions. The latter were distinguished in "easy" (e.g. 4 - 3), "difficult low" (e.g. 4.96 - 3.97) and "difficult high" (e.g. 4.97 - 3.96). Participants were asked to indicate their perceived magnitude. The experiment revealed that discounts were perceived as larger if the computation was easy compared to either difficult condition. This effect neither diminished with increasing size of magnitude nor changed when the scenario was framed as price difference between two competing stores or between regular and sale price. However, if participants were no longer required to perform the subtraction on their own – for example, when an ad displays the results of the calculation already: "regular: $5, sale: $4, you save: $1" – the ease-of-computation effect disappears.

In summary, help customers with computing discounts by choosing numbers and arithmetic that is less taxing on brainpower. Make it easier for customers to calculate price differences, for example, between regular and sales price ("$3 / $1 instead of $2.99 / $0.99"), but do not provide the result.

Marginal Price Difference Effect

Consumers can become overwhelmed and paralyzed by too many choices.

Iyengar and Lepper (2000) ran an experiment in a supermarket where they set up a table on which they displayed either six or 24 different jams. The researchers found that a large set of options attracted more attention (24 jams: 60% of customers stopped, six jams: 40%).

However, when it came to purchase decisions only 3% of customers who stopped actually bought compared to 30% when the selection was limited.

Looking into reasons why people have difficulties with choice Sagi and Friedland (2007) discovered that difficulty increases the more options to choose from and the less similar options are perceived. Larger choice sets and options that are more diverse instill a greater feeling of potential regret if a chosen option would not turn out satisfactorily. This expected regret makes consumers postpone decisions.

How can pricing increase similarity among options? The counterintuitive answer is through marginal price differences to otherwise similar options. Kim, Novemsky, and Dhar (2013) reasoned that consumers evaluate similarity between options by cancelling those attributes out that are identical and averaging those that are not. For example, a pack of gum is characterized by taste, units and price. If units and price were identical then consumers would only compare taste and might find that this gum is similar in one attribute. Now assume that the prices differ slightly by one cent. This difference draws consumers' attention so that it is evaluated whether it is similar to the competing option. In this case, the gum is now judged as similar in two attributes – taste and price – so that an increase in similarity would enhance likelihood that a customer makes a purchase decision. Kim, Novemsky, and Dhar (2013) ran this gum experiment in South Korea. Participants were given W1,000 (about $1) and asked which gum they would like to buy. Participants could also choose to keep the money and not buy any gum. When both gums were priced at W630 only 46% of participants decided to buy one of both options, but when the price was slightly different (W620 vs. W640) this proportion increased to 77%.

Adjust prices of similar options so that they are slightly different and support customer choice.

Phonetic Design

Name-Letter Effect

If your name is Thomas or Tiffany, are you aware that you subconsciously prefer numbers two and three to four and five?

Coulter and Grewal (2014) recruited 120 participants for an experiment whose last name started with either "E" or "T." The participants were exposed to a radio commercial about a bicycle of a fictitious brand. The researchers chose two prices sharing the same letter with the last name of the participant. In this experiment, they randomly assigned subjects to an ad mentioning either a price of $688 ("E" cue: six eighty-eight) or a price of $622 ("T" cue: six twenty-two). Consumers were asked to indicate their purchase intentions on a scale from one to seven. The experiment showed that consumers having their last name starting with "E" exhibited a 27% higher purchase intention at the higher price of $688 than at the lower price of $622. The opposite was true if a participant's last name began with a "T": people were more inclined to buy the product at a price of $622 compared with a price of $688. The boundary condition of this finding is that consumers actually have to hear or (internally) rehearse the price. In an additional field study, the researchers analyzed 275 car sales sold to customers carrying a first name beginning with the same letter as any digit (i.e. "O", "T", "F", "S", "E" and "N"). After the sale, those customers participated in a customer survey and rated their satisfaction with the deal they made. When the researchers regressed the number of digits matching the customer's name on their satisfaction rating, they found a statistically significant impact between price-letter-name-letter matching and satisfaction rating.

People evaluate prices more favorably if they contain a phonetical cue to the beginning of their own first or last name.

Syllables Effect

When processing Arabic numbers, consumers have learned that additional digits usually increase the magnitude of a number. More digits in general come along with more syllables so that customers associate more syllables with larger numbers (Brysbaert 1995).

Coulter, Choi, and Monroe (2012) demonstrated in a series of experiments that this syllables effect also holds for prices. We turn to what the research team calls "the Comma N' Cents effect" in the following.

To recognize syllables you have to actually pronounce words. The caveat is that the syllables effect requires consumers being either externally (e.g. ad commercial) or internally (e.g. internal rehearsal when writing a check) exposed to the verbal format of the price to be effective (Vanhuele, Laurent, and Drèze 2006).

Mind the number of syllables of your spoken price: Consumers perceive prices with fewer syllables as lower.

Comma Effect

Have you ever thought about whether the same price ($1645) appears smaller when pronounced as sixteen forty-five instead of one thousand six hundred forty-five)?

To manipulate the number of syllables of a given price Coulter, Choi, and Monroe (2012) introduced a comma into the same four-digit price and let it mention in a radio commercial as, for example, $1,645 (one thousand six hundred forty-five: 9 syllables) vs. $1645 (sixteen forty-five: 5 syllables). Then participants were asked to rate the magnitude of the price on a 10-point scale.

Participants rated the magnitude of the price with the comma higher than the same price without a comma.

The same effect occurs when participants were not verbally but visually presented with different versions of the same price and asked to remember the price for a few seconds. In this experiment, participants internally rehearsed the price number and rated a comma price higher than the same price without a comma.

Leaving out the comma in a four+ digit price reduces customers' price magnitude perception.

Cents Effect

The syllables effect described above also applies to the cents effect: the more syllables a price number requires, the larger is the perceived price.

To increase the number of syllables researchers added cents to the same four-digit price – e.g. $1645 (sixteen forty-five: five syllables) vs. $1645.48 (eight syllables). In an experiment, this price was announced in a radio commercial and participants were asked to rate their perceived price magnitude on a 10-point scale. Participants gave the price ending in cents a higher rating than the rounded price.

What about adding comma and cents to a price – the Comma N' Cents effect? As commas and cents independently increase magnitude perception, the combination of both lets customers perceive prices as higher than with a comma or cents alone. For example, participants perceived the level of the prices $1662 (no comma, no cents), $1662.91 (no comma, cents), $1,662 (comma, no cents), and $1,662.91 (comma and cents) on average as 5, 5.83, 5.58 and 6.50 on a 10-point scale.

Chopping of cents reduces customers' magnitude perception by more than the slightly lower monetary value suggests.

Phonetic Symbolism Effect

As shown above, syllables exert an influence on how consumers perceive prices, but how do smaller linguistic parts of a word – like phonemes – affect price perception?

In a classic study, Sapir (1929) found that people associate specific phonetic sounds with the concept of largeness or smallness. For example, people usually perceive back vowels (like "u" in food) and stops ("p," "k," "b") as large and front vowels (like "e" in test) and fricatives ("f," "v," "z") as small. This subconscious process of associating meaning to phonemes is called phonetic symbolism.

Related to prices, specific numbers carry different meanings depending on their pronunciation. For example, in the English language the number 2 consists of a back vowel and a stop and should be related to largeness whereas the number 3 is the opposite case.

Based on the congruency effect Coulter and Coulter (2010) tested the hypothesis whether a smaller sale price would be perceived as smaller if the phonetic sound of the sale price is related to smallness instead of largeness. In an experiment, the researchers exposed subjects to the same ad and just changed regular prices ($3 or $10) and sale prices. The researchers selected a product with a broad range of reasonable regular prices: an ice cream scoop. Participants were asked to read every price they would encounter without speaking aloud. Using regular prices of $3 / $10 the researchers presented sale prices of $2.33 / $7.66 (front vowels/fricatives = small) or $2.66 / $7.22 (back vowels/stops = large).

When subjects were asked to rate their perceived discount, they gave the "front vowels/fricatives" combinations higher ratings than for "back vowels/stops" prices – although the objective discounts were larger for the latter cases. Consumers overestimate discounts if the sale price is phonetically related to small. In English, this is the case for the numbers 3, 6, 7 and 8. One and 2 are typically associated with largeness. This effect only works if consumers verbalize the price. When participants were not asked to read prices for themselves the perceived discount reflected the true objective price discount.

Of course, these findings are only valid for numbers pronounced in English. In Spanish, use one, two, four, and eight for regular prices and three, six, and seven for sale prices. In Chinese, include two, five, eight, and nine for regular prices and one and seven in sale prices (Coulter and Coulter 2010).

To maximize perceived differences between regular and sale prices, use numbers 1 and 2 for regular prices, and numbers 3, 6, 7, and 8 in sale prices (English only).

Visual Design

Congruency Effect

An interesting question in the space of pricing is how do people mentally handle numbers? According to Dehaene's (1992) triple-code model, people encode numbers in general and price in particular in three ways: as Arabic number form (e.g. "13"), as auditory verbal version (/thirteen/), and as analogue magnitude code on a mental line (you can think of a point on line running from left to right). The latter can be stored as concrete number or as categorical evaluation like "small" or "large" (Monroe and Lee 1999).

Studies in numerical cognition showed that people could more easily differentiate numbers when external cues supported the comparison – i.e. cues were congruent with the value of each number.

For example, when the larger of two numbers is displayed in larger font size and, thereby, relates to the concept of "largeness," people require less time to differentiate both numbers compared to a neutral (same font size) or incongruent (smaller number in larger font size) situation (Henik and Tzelgov 1982). This effect is termed "size congruency effect."

In another experiment, Tzelgov, Meyer, and Henik (1992) asked participants to choose either the larger or the smaller of two digits. When the digit pair was small (two and four), people required less time to identify the smaller digit than to pick the larger. When the digits were large (six and eight), subjects took less time to identify the larger than the smaller digit. The impact of different frames of instructions and size of stimuli on response time is described as "semantic congruency effect."

Overall, if accompanying cues highlight the relative magnitude of each of two numbers, people can more easily differentiate both and perceive the distance as larger (Coulter and Coulter 2005). In the context of prices, this congruency effect is particularly important when comparing, for example, a sale price to a regular price. The following sections illustrate the congruency effect in action.

Consumers perceive a distance between two numbers as larger if the numbers' magnitude presentation is congruent with their value.

Font Size Effect

A common marketing tactic is to stress a low sale price with a larger font size. However, is this practice well advised?

As discussed above, studies demonstrated that people require less time to tell which number is larger if the larger (or smaller) of two numbers is also written in larger (or smaller) font size (Monroe and Lee 1999). How can we apply what is called "size congruency effect" to the presentation of prices?

In an experiment, Coulter and Coulter (2005) showed participants advertisements with a standard price and a reduced sale price. When the lower price was actually set in smaller font, participants perceived the sale price as significantly lower and were more willing to buy the product than in the incongruent condition – i.e. smaller sale price in larger font size.

Consumers show a higher purchase likelihood if the smaller sales price is displayed in a smaller rather than larger font.

Red Ink Effect

Are you seduced by red-colored prices in advertisements? If you are a male, the likelihood is rather high.

People use one of two routes to process information for decision making: systematic or heuristic processing (Chaiken 1980). Systematic decisions are those that people thoroughly evaluate and consciously make. On the on other hand, when we follow a rule of thumb and apply an educated guess, we engage in heuristic decision making.

Puccinelli et al. (2013) present the following reasoning: The first route of decision making requires more cognitive effort whereas the second works as a mental shortcut. Which route people follow depends on the level of involvement in a decision. Research showed that men are less involved when processing advertisements so they rely rather on heuristic cues when judging advertised offers (Meyers-Levy and Maheswaran 1991).

To test the hypothesis that men would rather rely on heuristic cues when evaluating advertised offers, the research team presented retail ads with toasters and microwaves to participants in an experiment. As semantic cue, the prices were colored in red, while the rest of the writing was in black. In the no-cue condition, the prices were also in black. If prices were in red, men rated perceived savings as higher than with black prices. In a similar experiment, the research team showed that male customers also associate more positive emotions with red prices compared to black. However, if men were highly involved in evaluating ads, the red color effect diminished.

By the way, female participants were immune: for red and black prices, there was no difference in perceived savings or degree of positive emotions across all experiments.

Present prices in red color to male customers.

Physical Distance Effect

Should you keep the higher regular price close to the lower sale price to stress that the offering is a good deal?

Coulter and Norberg (2009) developed the hypothesis that a congruent physical distance between prices actually mirrors perceived distance between price values. The researchers build upon studies in numerical cognition research that people tend to map magnitudes on an internal, analog scale that extends from left to right (Dehaene 1992).

In multiple experiments, Coulter and Norberg (2009) showed that participants could more easily tell (measured by response time) which of two numbers is larger if the physical space between those were larger as well. The researchers extended these findings to the context of prices and presented subjects with advertisements showing regular and sale price with either small or large horizontal distance. Supporting their hypothesis, participants expressed a greater willingness to buy when the physical distance was large. However, the effect did not materialize when prices were vertically separated. The internal magnitude scale extends from left to right; hence, vertical separation is not congruent with an internal perception of differences in numbers.

Display regular and sale price with larger physical distance – horizontally, not vertically.

Subtraction Principle

When displaying a regular and corresponding sale price does it matter whether you place the sale price to the left or to the right of the regular price?

Biswas et al. (2013) suggest that people perform subtractions more easily when the larger number is on the left and the smaller on the right. An experiment on general subtraction tasks confirmed this hypothesis. In the context of prices, researchers conducted an experiment during which participants evaluated a sale price of $309.99 (discount 30%) for a Blu-ray player in light of a regular price of $349.99. When the sale price was to the right of the regular price, respondents were more likely to buy the product than when it was on the left.

When the discount was reduced to 10%, this effect diminished. When a price is on sale without any information on the regular price, consumers assume a discount of between 10% and 12% anyway (Blair and Landon Jr. 1981) so that relative positioning of sale price to regular does not impact discount perception when the discount is low.

Summarizing, position prices you want customers to compare in the same way people would prefer when calculating differences in general: large number on the left-hand side, small number to the right.

Place lower (sale) price to the right of the higher (regular) price.

Horizontal versus Vertical Positioning

Choi and Coulter (2012) discovered that consumers tend to process discounts in relative (percentage) terms when reference and sale price were presented vertically (column-wise: higher reference price above lower sale price) and perceived discounts in absolute terms when displayed horizontally (side-by-side: higher reference price on left hand side).

The researchers also found that consumers prefer to compare prices between competing stores relatively and sale prices within the same store by the absolute price difference. Other studies showed that price discounts for low-priced items should be expressed as percentage discount, whereas absolute discounts are more effective for high-priced items. You'll find more details in this book in the section "Relative vs. Absolute Discounts."

In summary, when comparing your own sale price to competitive offers or regular and sale price for low-priced items, it is recommended to display reference and sale prices vertically. If high-priced items are discounted, present regular and sale price side-by-side with the regular price on the left. [See also section on "Subtraction Effect."]

A more recent study confirms this beneficial effect of vertically presenting own sales price below a regular price as this means of presentation reduces cognitive efforts required to calculate the offered discount (Feng et al. 2017).

As an interesting side note (Barone, Lyle, and Winterich 2015): Consistent handers – people who consistently use their left or right hand most of the time – expressed greater purchase likelihood when regular and sale price were displayed vertically for small discounts (in this experiment: $6.75 instead of $7). For large discounts (sale price $5 instead of $7) layout did not matter. Inconsistent handers – people who switch hands depending on the task – were more likely to buy when the discount is large and the layout is horizontally oriented. For small discounts, purchase likelihood was irrespective of layout.

When comparing competitors' prices to your own sale prices (for low-priced and high-priced products) or regular prices to sale prices (only low-priced products) display prices vertically (column-wise). For high-priced products present regular prices and sale prices horizontally.

Myth Debunked: Currency Sign Effect

You invite your spouse to an upscale restaurant. When you open the menu you notice that prices are written in a stylish font but lack a currency sign. Does this presentation influence our willingness to pay? You might have read about an experiment that confirmed a positive impact on price acceptance if currency signs are dropped. Let us take a closer look at the respective study.

Yang, Kimes, and Sessarego (2009) analyzed the impact of currency signs in price presentations. The research team reasoned that displaying dollar signs next to prices increases the salience of prices by subconscious priming. The researchers conducted an experiment in a restaurant context. Two kinds of menus were handed out to guests: In terms of content, these menus were identical but differed the way prices were displayed. Half of the menus contained just figures (e.g. "20") the other half added a dollar sign to the price (e.g. "$20").

Results showed an increase in spending of 8.15% (from $23 to $24.87) per person when the menu contained no currency sign, but this difference turned out to be statistically not significant.

The authors concluded "changing the menu typography is like picking the low hanging fruit when it comes to squeezing every last cent from an existing business: the yield may not be large, but it is easy to do (...)." (Yang, Kimes, and Sessarego 2009, p. 159).

Despite common beliefs, a currency sign next to a price (or absence thereof) does not significantly impact customer behavior.

Sale Prices and Discounts

Base Value Neglect Effect: Discount vs. Bonus Pack

When you are considering running a promotion, should you provide a price discount or increase product content at the same price?

A price discount of 20% is economically equal to a volume increase of 25%. Chen et al. (2012) discovered that consumers err when calculating percentages and tend to ignore the base value the percentage refers to – an effect coined "base value neglect."

The researchers observed that consumers systematically prefer a large percentage to a small percentage. This means consumers prefer a bonus pack to an economically identical price discount when both are expressed as percentages. Vice versa, consumers also prefer a size decrease to price increase when presented as a percentage.

In a field study, Chen et al. (2012) sold a hand lotion either at a 35% price discount or as bonus pack with 50% more content in a small retail store. After 16 weeks of promotion, the researchers observed that the bonus pack promotion sold 81% more units per day than the price discount promotion.

The researchers also identified factors when the base value neglect effect was more prominent. Consumers become indifferent between price discount and bonus pack when percentages are small or easy to convert (50% off versus 100% more). When customer face unfamiliar products, they prefer a price discount to a bonus pack when percentages are the same. For high-priced products, consumers react economically more rationally and favor the price discount over the bonus pack.

Consumers prefer larger product sizes to price discounts when expressed as a percentage.

Free Premiums for Unrelated Products

To buy food for your beloved puppy, you go to your trusted pet shop and see that the Innova brand is on promotion. Would you rather be enticed to buying when the promotion is a $1.99 price discount (regular price: $10.99) or a free can opener?

Nunes and Park (2003) suggest that consumers evaluate products separately if they cannot convert them into a common currency. When consumers evaluate two incommensurate products individually, prospect theory suggests that the total value of these segregated gains is larger than the value of combining both gains. Consumers automatically integrate outcomes that can be easily converted into a common unit of measurement (price discounts, larger package size, price for freebie displayed).

In other words, giving can openers for free should result in higher demand than a monetarily equal price discount.

The researchers found a cooperative pet shop and ran this promotion for three months offering both large (regular price $10.99) and small (regular price $6.99) cans at a price discount of $1.99 or with a free can opener. The can opener could be purchased for $1.99 in the same store, but it was not located close by the promotion stand.

In relative terms, the discount for the small can was 28% and for the large one 18%. When the promotion featured a price discount, demand significantly went up for small cans, but for large cans, this price discount was not sufficient to stimulate sales. Offering a free can opener had the same positive effect on sales as the price discount had for small cans. But this time, the free can opener also drove sales for large cans.

This experiment supported the rationale that adding an incommensurate freebie to a focal product leads to better value perception than an economically identical price discount.

If you wonder how you should design the corresponding advertisement, keep the following advice in mind that Raghubir and Celly (2011) developed: the picture of the free product on the ad should be small relative to the focal product otherwise quality perception of the focal product and purchase intent suffer.

If the monetary value of your price discount is relatively small then consider giving away a free, unrelated product instead.

Relative vs. Absolute Discounts

You discount a product from $80 to 65$. How would you frame the discount – as "$15 off" or "19% off"?

Research has repeatedly shown that consumers decide differently when the same absolute discount relates to different base prices (Chen, Monroe, and Lou 1998; Grewal and Marmorstein 1994; Lowry, Charles, and Lane 2005).

Tversky and Kahneman (1981) demonstrated this effect in an experiment. Participants read the following scenario: "Imagine that you are about to purchase a jacket for ($125) [$15], and a calculator for ($15) [$125]. The calculator salesperson informs you that the calculator you wish to buy is on sale for ($10) [$120] at the other branch of the store, located 20 minutes' drive away. Would you make the trip to the other store?" When the discount was 33% ($5/$15), 68% were willing to make the drive, but only 29% at a discount of 4% ($5/$125).

Chen, Monroe, and Lou (1998) showed that discounts for small-price items should be expressed in relative terms (percent), whereas consumers prefer absolute discounts on high-priced items. Lowry, Charles, and Lane (2005) identified a mid-price segment for which either discount presentation results in the same deal perception. As rule of thumb, one should choose the presentation frame depending on which frame results in a larger discount amount. This leads to a threshold price of 100 (irrespective of currency). If the regular price is higher than 100, an absolute discount is preferable over an equivalent discount stated as a percent and vice versa.

DelVecchio, Krishnan, and Smith (2007) investigated the long-term impact for relative versus absolute discounts beyond the sale period. The researchers found consumers have higher price expectations after the sale period if the discount is framed as a percentage. In other words, the consumer's internal reference price does not decrease as much in the percent discount frame as it does when the discount is presented as absolute amount.

> *If the regular price is below $100 express the discount as percentage, otherwise present the absolute amount of discount.*

Discounts and Tensile Claims

You plan a sale campaign and you have two economically equal options: offering a range of discounts from 10% to 40% or giving a straight (objective) discount of 25% for all sale items. Which option should you use? If you decide for a range of discounts, how should you frame it?

In terms of frames, there are three options with tensile claims:

- Present minimum savings ("Save x% or more"), hereafter "min frame"
- Present maximum savings ("Save up to y%"), hereafter "max frame"
- Present range of savings ("Save x% - y%"), hereafter "range frame"

Biswas and Burton (1993, 1994) discovered how consumers perceived savings from various discount frames and developed following recommendations. Given the same midpoint of your promotion (e.g. 25%), the researchers found:

- For wide ranges of promotions (e.g. 5% to 45%, 10% to 40%) consumers perceived savings as greater for a max frame relative to a min frame and range frame.
- For small ranges of promotions (e.g. 20% to 30%) subjects preferred a min frame over a max frame or range frame; however, consumers expected average discounts being lower than midpoint (16.64% to 21.63% < 25%) so that an objective discount

set at midpoint suggests a better deal for small ranges of promotions.

- Comparing an objective discount ("Save 25%") to a tensile claim, consumers perceived max frames as the best deal. Consumers perceived savings from an objective discount as higher than from a min frame ("Save 10% or more") or a range frame ("Save 10% - 40%"). But the max frame ("Save up to 40%") led to greater perceived savings than any of the other tensile or objective frames.

- Overall, a max frame is consistently related to higher purchase intentions (regardless of discount level).

- The authors cautioned that the highest discounts should not only be available for a limited share of selection or for unattractive products in order to avoid perception of deceptive behavior.

The explanation for these effects is anchoring and adjustment (Biswas and Burton 1993, 1994). Consumers anchor at the first number they encounter and adjust their evaluation from there.

When offering a wide range of discounts, use a max frame ("Save up to x%"), otherwise consider an objective discount.

Discount Frames and Proximity

You run a price promotion for an orange juice brand. Which discount frame should you choose (cents off, percentage off or revised priced)? And where do you place the sticker that communicates the new price – on the shelf, the shelf above, or on the product?

DelVecchio, Lakshmanan, and Krishnan (2009) built on research that shows consumers require considerable mental effort to calculate relative discounts in contrast to absolute discounts (Estelami 2003). So their researchers tested the impact of three discount frames on consumers' price perception: percentage-off ("25% off"), cents-off ("50 cents off"), and revised price ("Now $2.50").

In the context of low-priced, fast-moving consumer goods, the researchers reasoned that the mental effort required to calculate a discounted price is lowest for revised prices, higher for cents-off discounts and highest for percentage-off discount. Therefore, perceived prices are expected to correlate with mental effort. Furthermore, the researchers suggested that a discount message next to a price tag supports calculation of the discount as spatial proximity of both sets of information frees up resources in a subject's working memory.

DelVecchio, Lakshmanan, and Krishnan (2009) observed that consumers distinguished lowest discount prices as they predicted: revised prices were perceived as lowest, followed by cents-off frames and percentage-off frames.

Furthermore, the researchers also changed physical distance of discount message and regular price in three ways: they placed the discount tag either on the same shelf as the product, on the shelf above the product, or on the product itself. They found that physical distance does not affect discount perception for revised prices, but improved deal perception for cents-off and percentage-off frames.

In summary, (at least for FMCG) present price discounts as revised prices. If this discount message is technically not possible for a larger selection, place a percentage-off or cents-off message close to the regular sale price.

Communicate price discounts as revised prices (at least for FMCG). If this is not possible, place your cents off / percentage-off message close to the regular price.

Sequential Discounts

Imagine you have to decide between two offers: "25% off list price plus a special bonus of 25%" or "40% off list price". Which discount is more appealing?

Chen and Rao (2007) looked into this question and found that consumers prefer multiple discounts (25% off plus additional 20%) compared with an economically identical but percentage-wise lower single discount (40%).

This effect is explained by the base neglect effect as described in the previous section: As a rule of thumb, consumers just add up percentages and are less likely to engage in exact calculations. Prospect theory could also explain this effect as hedonic framing suggests segregating gains. More on this theory in section on "Prospect Theory and Value Function."

Consumers prefer a sequence of smaller discounts to one equivalent, larger discount.

Comparison to Regular Price vs. Competitor Price

Imagine you are about to create an advertisement for an upcoming sale. You have to decide whether to contrast your sale price to your regular price or to a competitive price. Which reference price would you choose?

It depends on the context of the customer's journey (Grewal, Marmorstein, and Sharma 1996). If customers were at home, a comparison to other competitors would reduce their need to search elsewhere. Nevertheless, when customers are already in a store, consumers prefer confirmatory information to justify their purchases. In this case, comparison to previous prices should be more effective. However, if discounts are particularly small or large, the type of cue is not expected to matter anymore.

The researchers conducted an experiment and asked participants to imagine they were either at home or at a store and saw an advertisement claiming either "Compare at $X. Sale price $Y." (between-store comparison) or "Regular price $X. Sale price $Y." (within-store comparison). First, the researchers demonstrated that this type of cue only exerts an influence when the price difference was moderate ($34.99/$24.99) but not when it was low ($29.99/$24.99) or large

($49.99/$24.99). The researchers found when customers are in a store, the comparison of a sale price to a regular price increased perceived value of a deal relative to a between-store comparison. Although the researchers showed that consumers on average prefer a between-store comparison when they are at home, they could not confirm that this difference was statistically significant in this study. A second, follow-up study finally confirmed the positive impact of between-store comparison cues when customers are at home.

A study conducted by Krishnan, Biswas, and Netemeyer (2006) explained why the researchers initially did not detect a difference. Krishnan, Biswas, and Netemeyer (2006) analyzed concreteness of a cue as a critical factor. The researchers asked subjects to imagine they were at home and evaluated an advertisement. The price comparison was manipulated by concreteness of cues and by comparison standard (between-stores versus within-store):

- "Circuit City Price $349, Our Price $299": concrete, between store
- "Regular price $349, Sale Price $299": concrete, within-store
- "Seen Elsewhere for $349, Our Price $299": abstract, between store
- "A $349 value, Sale Price $299": abstract, within-store

The researches revealed that between-store comparisons perform better when customers are at home only if the cue is concrete. For abstract cues, it does not matter which form of cue is used. The original study just considered abstract cues for the between-store comparison.

Grewal, Roggeveen, and Lindsey-Mullikin (2014) further explored the impact of additional factors on effectiveness for these semantic cues: hedonic vs. utilitarian products, shopping alone vs. shopping with a companion, and shopping in-store vs. shopping online.

To summarize what their research has discovered:

- Within-store comparisons are only effective in stores when customers shop alone, otherwise the kind of cue does not matter (as a friend might provide experience and suggestion that "over-writes" the impact of the cue).

- Only utilitarian products exhibit difference in cue effectiveness (for hedonic products, price is less important than product features).

- Between-store comparisons work best if they are concrete and customers perceive them at home.

- When customers shop online between-store comparisons appear favorable, though the difference to a within-store cue is not statistically significant (with advent of online shopping, information about competitive prices might not reduce search cost as much as it did when the first study was conducted).

In physical stores, compare your current sale price to the regular price; outside your physical store (advertisements, online shop) compare your price to competitors. When comparing to competitors be concrete.

Multi-Item Sales Prices

When you put an item on sale, does it matter whether you promote it as single-unit price ("on sale – 50 cents") or multi-unit price ("on sale – 6 units for $3")?

Wansink, Kent, and Hoch (1998) ran an experiment involving 86 supermarket stores. They found when prices were expressed as multi-unit prices, sales went up by 32% on average compared with single-unit prices, despite the same discount and per-unit price. The context of this experiment was fast-moving consumer goods with single-unit prices ranging from $0.50 to $2.50 and multi-item prices encompassing two to four units.

When promoting FMCG items on sale, create multi-item bundles.

Discounts on Products of High vs. Low Quality

Should you discount your high-quality products at all?

Wathieu, Muthukrishnan, and Bronnenberg (2004) found that price discounts for high-quality products that consumers do not expect to compete on price make consumers more salient about price as a buying decision criterion. When customers place more weight on price, less expensive products might become reasonable product alternatives despite lower quality. The researchers showed that discounts on high-quality products drove customers to low-quality products but not vice versa.

Do not discount high-quality products.

Phasing Out Discounts

When planning your price discount campaigns, should you follow a binary hi-lo pricing path or consider gradually phasing out discounts? Gradually phasing out means that you return in multiple steps from a discount to a normal price level instead of directly jumping back.

Tsiros and Hardesty (2010) reason that phasing out discounts provides customers an upward price trend from which customers conclude higher prices in the future and anticipate greater regret of missing out on a good deal.

In experimental studies the researchers confirmed that a "steadily decreasing discounting" (SDD) strategy relative to hi-lo pricing results in greater anticipated regret of not buying, higher expected future prices, a higher willingness to pay, a greater likelihood to visit the retail store and overall higher revenue and profit. When applying this strategy to real purchase situations the researchers confirmed that SDD generated 29% higher revenues and 44% higher profits compared with average hi-lo pricing.

Phase out discounts in multiple increments instead of returning to regular prices in one big step.

Conditional Discounts

Assume you are a big fan of your national soccer team and the world championship starts in two weeks. You plan to buy a new projector. Riding on this upcoming event, two electronic stores offer your preferred device at the same list price of $600 but with different discounts: Store A gives you a straight discount of $90, store B promises you a discount of $450 if your national soccer team wins the world cup. Where do you buy your projector?

Ailawadi et al. (2014) studied consumer preferences for conditional or uncertain promotions that depend on the occurrence of certain events, like sports results (winning gold at the Olympic Games) or weather conditions (> 3 inches of snow on Christmas). The researchers found that those subjects are most attracted by conditional discounts who find entertainment value in those promotions, enjoy to gamble, perceive low-thinking cost, and are involved in the conditional event.

One main factor why those individuals prefer conditional promotions over certain price discounts is that consumers tend to overestimate the probability of desirable events (Babad and Katz 1991). Ailawadi et al. (2014) found that participants reported a mean probability of 58% whereas conventional market wisdom suggested only 20% (odds as evaluated by a major betting website). The event in question was Germany winning the European Soccer Championship in 2012.

In summary, as consumers overestimate probability rates, conditional promotions are more cost effective than traditional, certain rebates and should become part of a marketer's promotional arsenal.

A specific segment of customers prefers conditional discounts to certain price rebates. As these discounts are more cost effective, marketers might consider them as part of their promotional mix.

Novel Discount Presentation

In your favorite electronics retailer, you browse around and discover a new type of discount message: "Pay 60% of the regular price." Up to now, the retailer would have presented discounts as "Save 40% off the regular price." You are surprised and take a closer look.

Kim and Kramer (2006) studied how novel discount presentation impacts consumers' perceived savings and purchase likelihood.

The researchers discovered that "Pay x% of the regular price" ("pay frame") is perceived as relatively novel in the U.S. where "Save y% off the regular price" ("save frame") claims are perceived as common, but found it is the other way around in Hong Kong.

Kim and Kramer (2006) performed the same experiment in the U.S. and Hong Kong. Subjects were exposed to a discount presentation in either a "pay 60%" frame or "save 40%" frame.

Results demonstrated that subjects in the U.S. perceived the "pay frame" as relatively uncommon, perceived savings as higher, and were more inclined to buy compared to the "save frame" condition. Results for subjects in Hong Kong were reversed.

In summary, novel discount presentations attract customers and increase purchase likelihood.

Apply discount presentations that are experienced as novel (e.g. import or export discount practices across regions).

Partitioned Pricing

Price Perception of Partitioned Prices

We distinguish partitioned pricing from price bundling (Burman and Biswas 2007). Partitioned pricing refers to single products that require mandatory surcharges (e.g. shipping and handling fees). Price bundling relates to a multicomponent product that customers could either buy individually (e.g. PC plus printer) or at least choose whether to include it as part of the main product (e.g. freezer plus warranty).

We cover the single-product case first and proceed with multicomponent products afterwards.

To test the general impact of partitioned pricing on willingness to pay, Morwitz, Greenleaf, and Johnson (1998) asked participants in an experiment to bid for a jar full of pennies in a sealed-bid auction. Participants were randomly assigned to either written instruction: In the "no surcharge condition," respondents were informed that they would have to pay what they indicated on the form, whereas in the "surcharge condition" the instruction told them that an additional premium of 15% would be applicable. Respondents handed in their bid and what they believed was the total value of the jar full of pennies in a closed envelope. The experiment showed that respondents faced with partitioned pricing made total higher bids (bid + premium) than the control group (bid without premium). Results showed that consumers tend to neglect surcharges and underestimate total costs.

Similarly, Hossain and Morgan (2006) found that bidders on eBay pay total higher prices (product price + shipping cost) for products when shipping cost was set to $3.99 instead of $0.

To answer the question "can we always divide and prosper" Burman and Biswas (2007) looked deeper into the conditions under which partitioned pricing is most effective. The researchers presented participants in an experiment with products of identical total price but with different surcharges (reasonable vs. unreasonable). First, they found that consumers with low need for cognition (LNFC) – i.e. people who derive less joy from thinking than those with high need for cognition (HNFC) – do not react to price partitioning. This group of LNFC customers exhibited a similar willingness to pay regardless of whether the price was partitioned or combined. Second, for HNFC consumers, partitioned pricing positively affected willingness to pay if the surcharge was perceived as reasonable compared to a combined price. This finding reversed when an unreasonable surcharge was presented.

You should split up prices in product price and additional fees as long as consumers perceive the surcharge as reasonable.

Significance of Surcharges

Consumers tend to underestimate surcharges and, hence, evaluate partitioned price more favorably over bundle prices. Does this finding change with increasing surcharges? Sheng, Bao, and Pan (2007) assumed that increasing the level of surcharges lets consumers perceive the offer as more unfair so that consumers are less likely to purchase the product. The researchers presented participants in an experiment with three different surcharge levels (low: 10%, moderate: 30%, and high: 50%) of a base price of $49.95 for a CD Walkman. In this experiment, respondents perceived higher levels of surcharges as increasingly unfair, letting their purchase intention drop. Only when the surcharge was low were subjects more willing to buy the product at a partitioned price compared to a bundled price version.

Surcharges should make up a low share of the base price when used in partitioned pricing – otherwise leave prices bundled.

Relative versus Absolute Surcharges

When selling a product that requires shipping fees, should you present an aggregate price ("$81.75 including shipping"), present surcharges in absolute terms ("$68.99 plus $12.76 for shipping") or frame surcharges as percentage ("$68.99 plus 18.85% for shipping")?

Kim (2006) tested the hypothesis that customers would neglect the information that is difficult to process and concentrate on the information that is easier to access. Consumers experience more difficulty when they process proportions compared to raw units (Estelami 2003). Therefore, this experiment investigated the question whether surcharges should be better presented in absolute or percentage terms. Participants indicated a higher purchase intention when the surcharge was presented in percentage terms compared to the integrated price or with absolute surcharges. These results confirm earlier findings (Morwitz, Greenleaf, and Johnson 1998).

Are percentage frames always more attractive? Another research team investigated whether the magnitude of surcharge influences the effectiveness of percentage terms. Keeping the total price the same, Xia and Monroe (2004) revealed that percentage frames lead only to higher purchase intentions when the surcharge was low (6% of $1,200 for a desktop computer). When the surcharge was high (12%), purchase intentions did not differ between dollar and percentage presentation.

Present reasonable surcharges in percentage terms.

Font Size of Surcharges

Does the font size effect [see above] also hold for surcharges?

Kim (2006) found that separating surcharges from a base price does not improve consumers' price acceptance in all cases. He developed the hypothesis that salience of surcharge impacts purchase intentions and that a smaller font size is less salient. During an experiment, he showed participants three versions of the same ad, but changed the price. The price was either integrated (total price including shipping) or segregated (product price plus shipping) whereas in the latter condition the font size of the surcharge was either smaller (low salience) or of the same size (high salience) as the product price.

Participants expressed stronger purchase intentions for partitioned prices only when the font size was smaller than that of the product price. This means when the surcharge was more salient this study supported the integration of losses principle as introduced in section "Prospect Theory and Value Function."

By the way, this effect is not impacted by whether surcharges are presented in absolute or percentage terms – a smaller font size for surcharges is effective in both cases.

Present surcharges in a smaller font than the base price.

Multiple Surcharges

If you have multiple surcharges – e.g. sales tax and shipping fees – should you sum them up to one larger surcharge or keep them separate as smaller amounts?

In this experiment, Xia and Monroe (2004) asked participants to indicate their purchase intention when exposed to one of three scenarios: price not partitioned, one surcharge (12%), and two surcharges (6% + 6%). The researchers hypothesized that consumers would more likely process multiple surcharges than a single one, so multiple surcharges receive more weight in the buying decision process.

This experiment confirmed that customers were more likely to buy the product when surcharge was presented as one sum instead of two.

Combine multiple surcharges into one.

Reverse Price Partitioning of Surcharges

When you present a final total price to your customers that includes shipping and handling fees, should you call out that the price includes surcharges?

Xia and Monroe (2004) conducted an experiment and exposed participants to the same ad with the same total price, but in one of four versions: (a) no information about surcharges, (b) free shipping included, (c) 6% of price as shipping and handling fee included, and (d) $72 (equivalent to 6%) as shipping and handling fee included. Participants expressed higher purchase intentions in all conditions when information on included shipping and handling fees were provided, i.e. (b), (c), and (d).

However, the results did not indicate any difference among those three conditions. This approach – the researcher coined this tactic "reverse price partitioning" – had the same impact on purchase intentions as actual price partitioning.

The only difference was that actual price partitioning results in better trustworthiness of store perceptions.

If you display a final total price, state that this price already includes surcharges ("free shipping").

Prospect Theory and Value Function

Prospect theory is a general concept applicable when multiple prices are involved. As we are currently discussing price partitioning and following up with price bundling, we cover this theory here.

Imagine you go shopping. The first product you find and put into your basket is $2 more expensive than expected. How do you feel? Then you pick the second item, which is luckily $2 cheaper than last time. You pay and leave the store. How do you feel about the purchase overall? How would you have felt if both products were priced as expected?

Prospect theory provides a framework to predict in general the value people derive from purchases and transactions with quantitative outcomes (Kahneman and Tversky 1979).

People are attuned to perceive differences rather than absolute states. One would feel a current temperature as hot depending on the temperature one has adapted to as reference point (Helson 1964). Therefore, Kahneman and Tversky (1979) conclude people perceive outcomes as deviations, gains or losses, from a current status quo in relative terms instead of absolute difference. For example, a pay raise of $5,000 provides more value when you earn $50,000 instead of $75,000. The researchers developed an S-shaped value function to find the expected utility or value of outcomes recognized as gains or losses.

The value functions has three properties:

- The value function considers gains and losses instead of absolute states of, for example, wealth. Its origin is the reference point, the status quo.

- The value function implies diminishing marginal returns. If you get a pay raise and you manage to negotiate additional $1,000, an increase from the initially offered $1,000 to $2,000 adds more value than an increase from $10,000 to $11,000.

- Consumers are risk averse. Losing a certain amount generates a higher negative value than a gain of the same amount delivers a positive value.

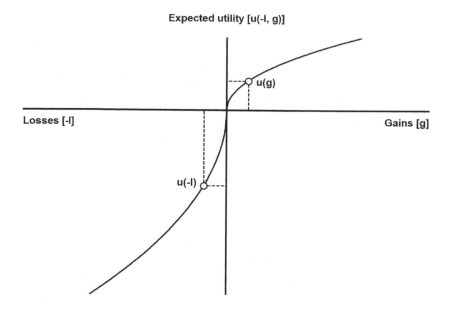

Figure 3: Value function (Kahneman and Tversky 1979)

The value function derives an expected utility (u) based on gains (g) and losses (-l). The following thought experiment illustrates gains, losses, and implied risk aversion. Assuming you are participating in a gamble and your bet is $10. Then a coin is flipped. If it shows head you win a certain amount ($x gain), if you lose your bet is gone ($10 loss). What is the minimum amount you need to win (gain) to participate in the gamble? Fully rational (not risk averse) decision makers would require at least $10.01 so that the expected, probability-weighted amount is greater than zero.

However, Tversky and Kahneman (1991) found that subjects require about 2 to 2.5 times their initial bet. In other words, losing $10 feels as bad as winning $25 feels good.

People engage in mental arithmetic so that they combine gains and losses that leads to maximum utility. They apply a set of rules in a process called *hedonic editing* (Thaler and Johnson 1990):

- Segregate gains: the total value of two individually evaluated gains is higher than the value of the sum of both gains, $u(g_1)$ +

$u(g_2) > u(g_1 + g_2)$. In a pricing context, this could mean to separate discounts.

- Integrate losses: the value of the sum of two losses is higher (though still negative) than the total value of two individually evaluated losses, $u(-l_1 + -l_2) > u(l_1) + u(l_2)$. This might suggest to bundle prices instead of showing them separately.

- Integrate (cancel) small losses with larger gains: because an amount considered a loss looms larger than the same amount perceived as a gain, losses should be cancelled, $u(-l + g) > u(-l) + u(g)$; $g > |-l|$. If you owe a cashback payment to a customer, but require a small administrative fee, it is beneficial to cancel the small fee and pay the remaining amount. The customer would be better off if she received just the net payment (cashback less handling fee) instead of the full amount and being required to make a small payment.

- Segregate small gains from losses: this is an edge case, also "silver lining." [See application to pricing in section "Silver Lining Principle: Trade-in Pricing."] Close to the reference point, the value function is particularly steep and flattens with increasing distance. If the gain is small relative to the loss, it could be the case that a small gain delivers a higher value than the equivalent reduction in losses would. In this case, segregation works: $u(g) > u(-l + g) - u(-l)$, $|-l| > g$. Silver lining suggests that a customer feels better if you charge a high price – for example, $1,200 for a new flat-screen TV – and give a small bonus of $50 in cash, compared with directly setting the price at $1,150.

Knowing these rules allows marketers to engage in *hedonic framing* to maximize consumers' expected value (Thaler 1999). A real-life example: In the course of discussion to shift costs for processing credit card payments to customers, officials of the credit card industry insisted that this price difference should be considered a cash discount instead of a credit card surcharge (Tversky and Kahneman 1981). Changing the reference point turns losses into gains and vice versa.

Consider gains and losses associated with your pricing and change your price presentation in a way that it helps customers maximize their perceived value. In the context of partitioned pricing prospect, theory suggests to aggregate multiple prices (losses) into a single amount.

Price Bundling

Price Perception of Bundled Prices

In this section, we use the term "price bundling" very broadly and cover three variations: product bundles, bundled products, and integrated products. The first case refers to separate, identical products that are sold together (e.g. multipack of soda). The second case means two or more individual products are sold as a package (e.g. PC and printer). In the third case, separate products are integrated into a new product (e.g. multimedia system). Other researchers are more specific and define the first as bundling, the second as price bundling and the third as product bundling (Stremersch and Tellis 2002, p. 57).

When presenting the price for a multicomponent product bundle, should you present one consolidated price or price each product component separately? In line with prospect theory, multiple prices could be seen as multiple losses. As the loss function is particularly steep for small losses (i.e. prices), consumers evaluate multiple smaller losses as worse than a one large loss of the same total amount. This theory recommends bundling prices in general (Thaler 1985) which was confirmed in subsequent studies (e.g. Drumwright 1992; Johnson, Herrmann, and Bauer 1999).

However, Engeset and Opstad (2017) conducted more nuanced research. The researchers studied how consumers perceived a multicomponent product bundle when the price for the bundle was either consolidated or itemized. This research was not about the question whether to bundle products but how to present prices for a given bundle. Participants imagined purchasing a weekend at a winter vacation destination and were exposed to either a two-item bundle (accommodation and ski-lift tickets) or a six-item bundle (accommodation, ski-lift tickets, train tickets, taxi from the train station to the hotel, taxi from the hotel to the train station, and dinner Friday and Saturday). Each bundle was priced either per item or in total. The researchers found that participants preferred itemized prices for large bundles but were indifferent between itemized and consolidated prices for small bundles. The reasoning behind this finding is that consumers form a more realistic price expectation for itemized prices that leads to more favorable offer evaluations.

For example, Johnson, Herrmann, and Bauer (1999) conclude that consumers perceive the highest value when discounts, considered as gains, are segregated and prices, considered as losses, integrated. The researchers confirmed this reasoning in an experimental study in the context of automobiles. Participants saw product features in three levels of aggregation (total price, base price + prices for feature packages, and base price + price for individual features) and with differently aggregated discounts (discount on total price, discount on feature packages, discount for individual features). When asked about their purchase intentions, respondents gave their highest ratings for the combination "bundled price with debundled discounts."

As general guidance, present the total bundled price and present gains for individual components (e.g. discounts) separately. If the bundle size is large (≥ six items) consider itemizing prices in a product bundle.

Nature of Secondary Product

The studies recommending price bundling referenced in the previous section held product benefits (gains) constant. How would customers react if this restriction was loosened?

Chakravarti et al. (2002) also referred to prospect theory and reasoned that product purchases consist of gains (i.e. product value) and losses (i.e. prices). The researchers argue consumers can easily add up individual prices so that the associated (negative) value of a single, consolidated price equals the value of multiple, smaller prices. The loss side of the mental account shows the same value for bundled and partitioned prices.

The research team tested the hypothesis whether price bundling versus price partitioning affects evaluation of gains (i.e. value derived from product components). According to prospect theory, multiple gains should lead to a higher value perception than one, consolidated gain.

Chakravarti et al. (2002) ran an experiment during which participants had to rate their likelihood to choose either of two offerings. The first offering was manipulated and the second held constant. The product offering consisted each of three components: a refrigerator coming with an icemaker and warranty.

The first offering presented three options. The first option was a bundled price ($499.95). The second and third options were each partitioned prices ($399.95 + $100) with either the icemaker or the warranty being separately priced.

The second, constant offer was described as a slightly smaller appliance with a bundled price ($429.95).

The researchers analyzed whether purchase likelihood for the first offering changed depending on price presentation. The experiment showed that consumers would prefer either partitioned pricing constellation to the consolidated price presentation. In addition, the researchers found that the type of partitioned product also impacts customer perception. If a consumption-related product (icemaker) was partitioned, consumers gave higher ratings than when a performance-related product (warranty) was separately priced.

This study concludes that consumption-related products tend to draw consumers' attention to the positive value derived from the product, whereas performance-related products potentially remind consumers on the negative possibility of failure of the product.

Debundle prices for consumption-related instead of performance-oriented components.

Performance of Secondary Product

For your upcoming holidays, you seek to book a flight. You have two options: Airline A offers a two-segment flight and takes almost eight hours at a price of $165. Airline B offers a direct flight taking roughly four hours at $205 for the flight and $10 for entertainment and food, i.e. one episode of a sitcom and refreshments. Which option would you choose? Would your decision change if Airline B just offered a bundled price of $215?

Bertini and Wathieu (2008) discovered that consumers place more attention on the secondary component if it is priced separately. Consequently, if consumers evaluate the performance of the secondary component as not attractive, they also perceive a partitioned price as less attractive than an all-inclusive price.

The researchers ran an experiment and asked subjects to choose between two options as described above. Airline A was held constant and was just described by the flight duration and price. Airline B offered either a "bad deal" (one episode of a sitcom and refreshments) or a "good deal" (six movie channels and full-service meal) on the secondary attribute. (The researcher actually confirmed that the subject considered the flight as primary attribute.) Furthermore, airline B priced the primary and secondary components separately or as one all-inclusive price.

Results from this experiment showed that consumers were more likely to choose the good deal when it was priced separately, but preferred the bad deal when it was presented as a combined price.

In other words, if your secondary attribute is underperforming, bundling prices increases purchase intentions. The opposite holds true if your secondary component is perceived as attractive.

Important to note, Bertini and Wathieu (2008) also found that the secondary attribute needs to be seen as secondary. If consumers perceive both attributes as equally important, the impact of different pricing frames does not affect purchase intentions any more.

If your secondary product component is outstanding then debundle prices; if it is underperforming, combine prices.

Price-Value Congruency in Price Bundles

Your car needs a new bumper and you receive quotations from two repair shops. Shop X charges $89.95 for the part and $32.50 for labor. Shop Y prices the bumper at $69.95 and takes $52.50 for labor. The total price is the same in both cases, $122.45, and the quality of the parts is identical as well. Which shop would you choose? Unfortunately, next month your headlights break. You receive following quotations. Shop X charges $39.95 for the headlights and $127.50 for labor. Shop Y prices $59.95 for the part and $107.50 for labor. The total price and the quality of the headlights are identical. Again, which shop would you choose?

Yadav (1994) suggests that consumers evaluate bundles by the component with the highest price. Following this rationale, consumers should choose shop Y in both cases.

Prospect theory (Kahneman and Tversky 1979) proposes to choose the option that has a lower price in the less expensive component. To explain this conclusion, we look at the bumper case example. The loss from a price increase in labor from $32.50 (shop X) to $52.50 (shop Y) is perceived higher than from $69.95 (shop Y) to $89.95 (shop X) for the spare part due to diminishing marginal changes in value. This reasoning suggests choosing shop X in the bumper and the headlights case.

However, Hamilton and Srivastava (2008) hypothesized that the nature of the components being partitioned and their relative prices determine customer preferences. The researchers argued that customers are less sensitive to price changes for product components that provide a high value. Conversely, consumers are expected to react more strongly to price changes in components that add little value. Holding the total bundle price constant, consumers should prefer the bundle with a relative low (high) price share for the low (high) benefit component. Hence, in the example above, the researchers expect that consumers will evaluate the value of labor as relatively low compared to the spare parts and predict that the subject would prefer shop X in the bumper case and shop Y in the headlights case. Hamilton and Srivastava (2008) tested and confirmed their prediction in an experiment.

In summary, when determining how to partition your product and what prices to set for each component, consider the relative value that your components provide your customers – instead of splitting partitioned prices proportional to your costs, for example.

Consumers prefer bundles with low prices for low value components and high prices for high value components.

Bundling Expensive and Inexpensive Products

Assume you are considering buying a new pair of Nike running shoes and an unbranded, inexpensive t-shirt – it is just for running anyways. When pondering how much you are willing to pay, you put a price tag of $150 for the shoes and $10 for the t-shirt. By pure coincidence, someone offers you both products as a bundle. What would be your willingness to pay? The sum of both individual amounts? Less than the sum? But definitely more than the more expensive of both (at least $150), right?

Indeed, Brough and Chernev (2012) found that typical customers would pay LESS for the product bundle than they would pay for the more expensive item if the price difference between bundled prices is large. The researchers found that consumers assign products of different price tiers to different categories. When asked about their willingness to pay for a whole bundle, consumers apply a process of "categorical averaging." The result of this process is more an articulation of perceived expensiveness than the summed value of individual products.

In multiple experiments, the researchers asked participants to indicate their willingness to pay for individual items and for the total bundle. When bundling an expensive and an inexpensive item, consumers' willingness to pay for the whole bundle was on average 25% below their willingness to pay for the expensive item when evaluated in isolation.

Never bundle inexpensive and expensive products.

Bundling Low-Tier and High-Tier Brands

You are about to buy a new MP3 player. You find two offerings, a player from Bose ($55) and a Sandisk player ($35), each with an FM radio plug-in accessory at no extra charge included. Which one would you choose? Would your choice change if prices were separated – i.e. Bose player priced at $40, Sandisk player at $20 plus a plug-in accessory at $15?

Love (2012) investigated the question of whether the quality of a brand impacts the attractiveness of a price bundle. The researcher proposed that high-tier brands profit from a halo effect that is highlighted when prices are partitioned, but diminishes when bundled. For low-tier brands, he followed the rationale of the mental accounting theory that suggests integrating losses (i.e. prices).

Based on multiple experiments and actual auctions on eBay, the researcher found that consumers exhibit a larger willingness to pay when prices for low-tier brand were bundled and prices for high-tier brands were presented separately.

Only bundle prices for low-quality brands and present prices for high-quality brands separately.

Discounts on Mixed Bundles

Research on bundling so far has focused on products that are related and frequently bought together. How does bundling of unrelated, cross-category products affect customer behavior?

Khan and Dhar (2010) looked into bundling hedonic and utilitarian products ("heterogeneous bundle").

When consumers consider buying hedonic products, they usually feel a greater sense of guilt and experience greater difficulty to justify a purchase compared to buying utilitarian products (Okada 2005). The researchers concluded that a discount on the hedonic product in a heterogeneous bundle helps justifying the purchase of the overall bundle. Therefore, they assume that a discount on the hedonic product part increases likelihood of purchase compared to allocating the same discount to the utilitarian product as the latter does not require much justification for purchase. However, if two hedonic products were bundled, a discount on either product would not sufficiently justify a purchase. Similarly, a discount on either of two utilitarian products would not be very effective, as it does not add much to the justification of buying the bundle.

Khan and Dhar (2010) asked participants to imagine they look up item X at an online retailer and found the company was offering a bundle deal to an equally priced, but unrelated item Y. One third of the participants were told that the retailer offered a discount of $20 on X, another third were told about a discount of $20 on Y, and the last third received no information about discounts. For X and Y, the researchers chose two hedonic (barbecue grill, fondue set) and two utilitarian products (office chair, printer). When randomly exposed to six different product bundles and three different discount frames, participants were significantly more likely to buy heterogeneous product bundles when the discount was on the hedonic product.

Combine utilitarian and hedonic products and place a discount on the hedonic component.

Customer Preferences in Discounted Price Bundles

If you offer a two-product bundle and plan to offer a discount on either product, which product should you choose? Does it matter whether the same discount is allocated to product A or B as long as the total price stays the same?

Yadav (1995) found that customers show different purchase intentions depending on which product a discount is offered. When the discount is offered on the more preferred product, consumers are more likely to buy the bundle. Participants were asked to indicate how likely they were to buy a bundle of two subscriptions, one magazine targeting the media segment (*People Weekly*), the other aiming at the sports segment (*Sports Illustrated*).

Results showed that participants were more inclined to choose the bundle that featured a discount for their preferred magazine.

In a price bundle, discount the product that your customers prefer.

Role of Reference Prices in Price Bundles

Janiszewski and Cunha Jr. (2004) dove deeper on the question how and why consumers react differently to price bundles when discounts were given for one component instead of the other, although total bundle price and total bundle discount did not change.

The researchers drew on the reference price model and reasoned that every consumer holds an internal reference price against which they compare a presented price. If the price of a bundle component exceeds the respective reference price, consumers experience a loss, otherwise they evaluate the offer as a gain.

As the value function is steeper for losses than for gains, the researchers argue that reducing losses is more valuable to customers than to increase gains by the same amount.

In multiple experiments, Janiszewski and Cunha Jr. (2004) showed that consumers preferred one product bundle over another when the discount that was given on the product exceeded the participants' price expectations.

For example, in one experiment, the research team presented a bundle of a pizza and 10 chicken wings. They surveyed respective reference prices in a pre-test: pizza $8.11 and wings $4.20. The participants were told that each product carries a pre-discount price of $7.99 and the bundled price received now a 50% on one item. When consumers were asked to choose between two bundles (Pizza $7.99 / 10 wings $3.99 or 10 wings $7.99 / pizza $3.99) the majority would decide in favor of the former (86%).

This finding supports the proposed theory: in the second bundle, the price for wings ($7.99 > $4.20) exceeded the participants' reference price so that it a led to a higher negative value although the total product bundle price was the same.

Linking this result to the previous section on customer preferences, the current findings suggest that a discount does not necessarily need to be allocated to a more important product in the eyes of the customer, but to the product customers perceive to be too expensive without a discount.

Discount the product component in the bundle that exceeds the customer's expected price without the discount.

Salience and Level of Discount in Price Bundles

When offering a discount on a bundle, should you point customers to the savings in any case? Does it backfire to stress a discount of a mere four cents on a burger combo meal?

Harris and Blair (2012) ran an experiment to figure out how customers react to different levels of a bundle discount when the discount was made more or less salient. The researchers argue that consumers perceive discounts as larger when they engage in piecemeal evaluation of individual component prices instead of holistic evaluation of the overall bundle. To trigger piecemeal evaluation, component prices should be made more salient to customers.

In this experiment, the research team presented participants with one of four versions of a realistic menu of a well-known, fast food chain. The menu contained one combo meal with a discount of either $0.04 or $1.04. In the more salient condition, prices of the individual products were displayed as part of the combo offer. For the less salient condition, the component prices were not included in the combo offer but available in other places of the menu. Participants were asked to place a realistic order. The researchers then analyzed whether the respondent had ordered the discounted combo meal. When individual product prices were less salient, the share of choosing the combo was about the same for the small discount and large discount condition. When the individual prices were made salient, the share of participants choosing the combo increased from 45% to 60% for large discounts but went down from 48% to 30% for small discounts. These results confirm the initial hypothesis, when component prices are made salient, consumers get more involved in processing and evaluating single item prices.

When offering a large discount make the individual product prices more salient. If the discount is small, keep prices of product components less salient.

Price Changes for Price Bundles

When prices for bundles change – increase or decrease – how should the price increase or decrease be best framed?

Mazumdar and Jun (1993) drew on prospect theory and reasoned that consumers consider price decreases as gains and price increases as losses. According to the aforementioned value function, losses should be integrated and gains be separated (Thaler 1985).

In the researchers' experiment, participants read about two geographically separated buyers, A and B. Both buyers bought the same two products but to buyer A the products were only available as a bundle, whereas buyer B could only buy both products separately. These buyers experienced price increases (or decreases) and participants were asked which buyer they think would be happier (or more upset).

Results confirmed that consumers prefer price decreases on multiple product components but feel better when price increases were consolidated on a bundle level.

When prices increase for some bundle components but decrease for others, prospect theory suggests that mixed gains (i.e. price decreases exceed price increases) and mixed losses (vice versa) should be summed up on a bundle level (Thaler 1985).

Heath, Chatterjee, and France (1995) experimentally confirmed these principles for absolute price changes. However, when price changes were expressed as percentages, consumers preferred segregation of discounts and price increases.

If expressed in absolute terms, communicate price increases on a bundle level (even if partially offset by price decreases for single components), but present price decreases for individual components. Always separate mixed price increases and discounts when presented as percentages.

Price-Unit Order for Packages

You are about to price a package of soda cans. The price point is about 50 cents per can and you plan to bundle about 40 units. Should you price them at "35 cans for $19" or "40 cans for $20"? On the other hand, why not change the order to "$19 for 35 cans"? For multi-item packages, you wonder whether order of prices and units actually matters.

Bagchi and Davis (2012) investigated the question of how consumers react differently to "$29 for 70 units" versus "70 units for $29".

The researchers reason that three parameters of packages can be changed in this context: presentation order (price-units vs. units-price), package size (10 units vs. 70 units) and calculation difficulty ($20 for 40 units vs. $19 for 35 units). When calculation difficulty is high and package size is large, the researchers argue, people tend to anchor on the first item of the package presentation. If the first item is the price, consumers insufficiently account for the number of units and typically perceive the package as more expensive. If the first item is the number of units, the opposite emerges. In addition, when calculation difficulty is high, consumers might apply heuristic evaluation and place more weight on the first information they encounter. However, these effects are only expected to occur when calculation difficulty is high and package size is large. If calculation difficulty is low, people should easily calculate per-unit pricing so the order of presentation should not matter. If the package size is small, the researchers assume that consumers translate more difficult calculations into easier approximate ones (e.g. $2.90 for seven to $3 for nine).

In multiple experiments Bagchi and Davis (2012) confirmed that order of price-unit presentation changes consumers' purchase intentions for large packages with a high difficulty of calculating price per unit. Results show that consumers prefer unit-price presentations over price-unit presentations and that consumer are indifferent when package size was small or calculation difficulty was low.

These finding do not suggest that large packages with units presented first lead to highest attractiveness ratings, indeed one study revealed that smaller packages with low calculation difficulty were perceived as having highest value.

In summary, research results recommend placing units first when package size is large and the per-unit price is difficult to calculate.

If per unit prices are difficult to calculate, place units before price (eg. "70 units for $29").

Bundling and Consumption

Imagine you are on a ski vacation and bought a four-day ticket in advance. After three fun, perfect days on the slopes, weather conditions change. A friend suggests leaving early to beat the traffic. Would you go skiing with your remaining ticket? What would you decide if you had prepurchased four single-day tickets?

Soman and Gourville (2001) argue that consumers experience a greater ambiguity when relating a single payment to multiple products compared to a single payment for each single product. Overall, costs are less salient for bundled products in contrast to unbundled products. As perceived (sunk) costs drive consumption, the likelihood to forgo consumption of bundled products is expected to be higher than of single products.

The researchers conducted an experiment and posed the introductory question to participants. Results showed that subjects were more likely to go skiing if they had prepurchased four single-day tickets instead of one four-day pass.

Bundling reduces likelihood of consuming prepurchased products.

Price Changes

Psychophysics and Just Noticeable Price Difference

Honestly, do you notice a minor price change especially for products you do not care about that much? And, if you noticed the price change, would it be material enough that it matters and you stay away from buying the product?

The way people notice changes to prices is similar to other physical stimuli like light, sound, or mass that is explained by Weber's law (Monroe 1971b): The just-noticeable change (ΔS) to a stimulus (S) is proportional to the base stimulus: $\Delta S / S = K$, where K is a constant.

This law stipulates that with increasing magnitude of a stimulus the change in stimulus needs to increase as well to be recognized. An additional five pounds to a barbell carrying 20 pounds would be noticed, but adding five pounds to 120 pounds might not be perceived.

Applying this law to prices as stimuli (Monroe 1973) concludes the existence of a *differential price threshold* that suggests a *just-noticeable difference* with implications for price changes and price comparisons. On the one hand, a differential price threshold means that prices can be increased without causing customer responses as long as price changes stay below this threshold. On the other hand, this threshold also equals the minimum discount or price drop you need to offer to stimulate sales. This differential price threshold (i.e. constant K) varies widely and depends on product categories, consumer characteristics (e.g. income), price levels (K tends to increase with increasing price levels) and other, still unstudied determinants. Cheng and Monroe (2013) summarized various empirical studies gauging K is about ± 6 to 10% for price increases. For price decreases, K can reach up to >30% for minimum discounts required to stimulate sales.

The existence of a just-noticeable difference and differential price thresholds suggests areas of constant and of highly elastic demand. Thinking in terms of a demand curve, we would expect "kinks" in its graph at the respective threshold values. Pauwels, Srinivasan, and Franses (2007) studied actual sales for four brands across 20 product categories and found kinks or threshold-based price elasticities for 76% of 80 brand-category combinations at historical prices, competitive prices or both price points.

The researchers also found asymmetric threshold values for gains, i.e. discounts, and for losses, i.e. price increases. For the study conducted, the threshold for gains was -16% and for losses +7%. In this study, a discount of 20% triggered a more than proportional increase in sales (simulated value: $2,120K) than a 10% discount ($640K).

Differential price thresholds describe ranges of prices where consumers are relatively insensitive to price changes.

Price Increases through Package Downsizing

If you downsize your product package as a means to raise a per-unit price, how would customers react and how should you actually change the package?

Çakır and Balagtas (2014) found that customers are less sensitive toward changes to package size than they are to price changes. The researchers estimate that the package size elasticity is roughly one-fourth of the price elasticity. Downsizing packages instead of raising prices might be the more profitable solution.

Chandon and Ordabayeva (2009) looked into consumers' perception of size and volume. They found that consumers systematically underestimate reductions in package sizes. Participants in an experiment perceived a reduction of 25% as 22% if applied to only one dimension (e.g. height). However, if the reduction involved all three dimensions (i.e. height, width, and depth) consumers perceived the reduction as only 17%. Conversely, if you plan to perform a promotion that offers a larger package size, then you should only increase the package size along one dimension.

What if your product has only two dimensions, like a pizza, or when customers see only one side of your box placed on a supermarket shelf?

Krider, Raghubir, and Krishna (2001) propose following recommendations to improve size perception of two-dimensional products:

- Use tall rectangular shapes instead of circular ones
- Present your rectangular shape standing on a corner (like a kite)
- Graphically highlight the longer of two dimensions (e.g. double-sided arrows)
- Numerically present the surface of your product (not just diameter or side sizes)
- Consider discounts on two small products (e.g. pizzas) instead of an equivalent discount on a large product version

Additional note: Research also shows that customers prefer a downsizing to an economically equal price increase. More on this effect in section on "Base Value Neglect Effect: Discount vs. Bonus Pack."

Customers are less sensitive to product downsizing than they are to price increases. Downsize your package along all three physical dimensions, but increase your package only in one dimension.

Price Level

Price-Quality Inference

Marketers may set prices at a higher level because consumers infer a better quality from higher prices. This effect is among the most researched phenomena in behavioral pricing and was already studied more than six decades ago (Leavitt 1954; Scitovszky 1944).

Völckner and Hofmann (2007) analyzed 71 studies from 23 publications spanning from 1989 to 2006. The researchers distilled following findings:

- The impact of price on quality perception is significant but has decreased since reported in the late 1980s (Rao and Monroe 1989).
- Price-quality inference is stronger for higher-priced products.
- Price-quality inferences decrease with increasing familiarity with the product.
- Price-quality inference is stronger for fast-moving consumer goods than for services or durable goods.
- Price-quality inference is stronger in European countries than in North American countries.

The researchers concluded that marketers should wisely decide about price levels and discounts. A price that is set too low, lowered over time or temporally discounted could serve as a signal of low quality that in turn hurts rather than stimulates sales.

The more information is available to a consumer to evaluate a product's quality, the less the effect of price on expected quality (Chang and Wildt 1996). However, this effect reverses when consumers become overwhelmed by information overload and so return to price as a signal for quality.

Interestingly, Cai, Tang, and Jia (2009) found that consumers in a negative mood are more likely to use price as a signal for quality and, thus, show a higher likelihood to buy expensive products than people in a good mood who focus rather on the negative side of high prices and prefer less expensive products.

Consumers use prices to infer the quality of a product. Hence, setting prices too low threatens quality perception so that higher prices potentially increase demand.

Placebo Effect

Price does not only influence expected quality before a purchase but also experienced quality after the purchase – the placebo effect.

McConnell (1968) served participants in an experiment three identical beers with different, fictitious brands at different prices. Consumers preferred the beer with the highest price. This effect was neuroscientifically confirmed. When subjects were positioned in a brain scanner (fMRI) and served the same wine at different prices, it was found that the brain area associated with pleasure was more active when the price was higher (Plassmann et al. 2008).

A higher price not only influences the perception of taste, it also affects actual performance. In an experiment, Shiv, Carmon, and Ariely (2005) let participants consume an energy drink. Half of the group was told that the energy drink was at full price; the other half learned that the energy drink was discounted. Then participants were asked to solve a series of puzzles. As the "full price" group expected higher performance – i.e. better stimulation of the brain – this group solved significantly more puzzles than the "discounted price" group.

A similar study confirmed this effect (Waber et al. 2008). Subjects in an experiment were given pain relievers that were either at full price or discounted. When participants were given electroshocks to their wrist, those who received full-price pills reported less pain than subjects who took pills at a discounted price.

Higher prices induce consumers to perceive product quality as better during actual consumption.

Pricing Mechanisms

Flat-Rate Bias

When considering your choices for your Internet access, mobile phone contract, pay TV subscription, health club plan or even your last (all-inclusive) holiday, did you decide on a flat-rate or did you pay per use? Which fee would economically have been a better choice?

Lambrecht and Skiera (2006) showed that consumers exhibit a flat-rate bias. This means people prefer a higher allowance instead of variable pay-per-use prices although the sum of pay-per-use payments would be lower than the flat-rate.

The researchers discovered three reasons explaining this flat-rate bias.

- Insurance effect: Consumers insure themselves against higher-than-expected payments.
- Taximeter effect: Consumers enjoy a product more if it is paid per flat-rate instead of per-use, similar to the ticking of a taximeter that reduces the joy of a taxi ride.
- Overestimation effect: Consumers overestimate their expected demand for a good.

In summary, this study demonstrated that a flat-rate tariff was more profitable for the company than any pay-per-use tariff, but also provided a better overall value to its customers at the same time.

For products or services, consider offering an economically attractive flat-rate tariff.

Trade-in Pricing

Your current sneakers are still in good shape and you actually still like them. But you find a new pair of your favorite brand on sale in two stores. The regular selling price is $75. Store A offers a sale price of

$65. Store B offers you to trade in your old pair for $10. How likely are you to accept either offer?

Okada (2001) developed the hypothesis that consumers open a mental account when buying a reusable product – also termed durable. In this account, people track their cumulative enjoyment and compare it to the price paid. The researcher termed the positive difference between price and cumulative benefits as book value. If the book value is positive, people experience a loss when they replace the product and close the account. Thus, a replacement decision is influenced by whether people felt they got their money's worth.

How does this theory inform the decision of whether a seller should offer a price discount or a trade-in value for the product to be replaced?

As discussed in the section "Prospect Theory and Value Function," losses loom larger than gains. Okada (2001) explained that people recognize a price discount as a gain and a trade-in value as reduction of loss. Therefore, people should prefer trade-in pricing to price discounts for reusable products. The researcher tested this hypothesis asking participants about their probability of replacement in light of a price discount versus a trade-in price for different situations of residual book value.

The findings were two-fold. First, the higher the book value the larger was the difference in replacement probability between sale price and trade-in offer. Second, overall, individuals were more likely to replace their old durable product when they were offered a trade-in value (76%) in comparison to a price discount of the same monetary value (66%).

In a second experiment Okada (2001) demonstrated that this effect reversed when the old durable still carried a value, either as a gift to someone else or with a monetary value on the market for used products.

To reduce the painful experience of closing mental accounts for durable products, the researcher concluded that mental accounting explains why apparel retailers offer to buy back old pairs of sports shoes or old suits when purchasing a new one.

People prefer trading in old reusable products over price discounts in particular if these products have no monetary value.

Silver Lining Principle: Trade-in Pricing

You are about to buy a new digital camera and trade in your old one. You found two stores that are willing to pay for your old digital camera. The first gives you $40 and charges you $250 for the new one; the second store values your old camera at $80 and sets a price of $290 for the new camera. In both case you pay $210 and give away your old camera. Which offer do you prefer – or are you indifferent? How would you decide if your old camera was worth $250?

Kim et al. (2011) analyzed this question and reasoned that consumers prefer to be overpaid on their trade-in good and overcharged for the new product if the ratio of trade-in value to new-product value is small. The preference reverses if the value of the trade-in product relative to the product to be purchased is large. The silver lining principle laid out in the section on prospect theory explains this behavior. People perceive trade-in goods as gains and prices paid for the new product as losses. If the gain is relatively small compared to the price to be paid for the new product, consumers tend to segregate gains and losses. As the value function is relatively steep for small gains compared to large losses, receiving additional dollars for the trade-in good delivers a higher value than additional dollars to be paid for the new product reduces value. On the other side, for relatively large gains (i.e. high trade-in value relative to price of new product), consumers prefer to integrate gains and losses.

The researchers ran an experiment that confirmed expected results. Participants preferred overpayment on a traded-in camera (trade-in value: $80 vs. $40) and overcharging on new camera price ($290 vs. $250) when the ratio of trade-in value ratio to new product price was small. When the respective ratio was high, preferences reversed: customers preferred a low price for the new camera (trade-in value $210 / new price $250) over a high price (trade-in value $250 / new price $290) holding the total price paid ($40) constant.

If you allow customers to trade in old products, consider overcharging on trade-in goods and overcharging on the new product if the value of the trade-in item is small relative to the new product's price.

"Pay What You Want" Pricing

Your friend invites you to a restaurant where you pay as you wish any amount, including zero. How much would you pay in comparison to a standard price that you usually pay for a comparable place? How likely is your visiting this restaurant again?

In essence, with pay-what-you-want (PWYW) pricing, you purchase a product or a service and pay any amount you want. Why should business owners consider this tactic?

Research on this new pricing mechanism is continuously growing and unearthed the following findings in terms of economic viability (e.g. Chen, Koenigsberg, and Zhang 2017; Kim, Natter, and Spann 2009, 2014; Krämer et al. 2017; Lynn, Flynn, and Helion 2013; Riener and Traxler 2012; Stangl, Kastner, and Prayag 2017):

- Only a few customers pay nothing or more than the regular price.
- The majority of customers pay less than the market price so that the average price is lower with PWYW compared to fixed-price pricing. (Side note: PWYW customer prefer to pay round prices.)
- It supports market penetration: The number of sales and customers increases with PWYW so that total revenue potentially increases compared to fixed posted prices. (There are examples

of restaurants successfully implementing this pricing mechanisms, but there are also counter examples.)

- PWYW is most beneficial for services (and products) with low
  variable costs, negligible capacity constraints, and spill-over effect on complementary products (common examples are ho-
  tels, restaurants, museums or digital music).
- As a promotional tactic, PWYW might be preferred to free
  sampling or price discounts depending on the marketer's objective: PWYW generates higher word-of-mouth and repeat purchase intentions compared to sampling or discounting.
- PWYW reduces price competition.
- PWYW helps to price discriminate between customers with
  different willingness to pay.

*Pay-what-you-want pricing is a new mechanism that appears prom-
ising for companies focusing on growth with low marginal costs.*

"Name Your Own Price" Pricing

Instead of paying whatever amount you wish, name-your-own-
price (NYOP) pricing asks potential customers to submit a bid and
compares it against a secret threshold (Spann and Tellis 2006). Only
when the bid is above the threshold does a transaction takes place. This
pricing technique was invented by Priceline, a company selling third-
party flights, hotel rooms, rental cars, and vacation packages (Anderson 2009).

Krämer et al. (2017) compared NYOP to PWYW pricing. The researchers found that NYOP is a less aggressive strategy in terms of market penetration, is attractive also for products with higher variable
costs, and is economically profitable due to the lower threshold of acceptable prices. NYOP can be applied concurrently to a high-price
strategy to attract price sensitive customer segments. Companies can
sell excess inventory via intermediaries through NYOP to price-con-
scious consumers, but still selling those products with posted prices to

value-oriented customers. In this way, NYOP helps companies segment the market by customers with different levels of willingness to pay without negative consequences on their brands.

Name-your-own-price pricing is a new participative pricing mechanism that draws on the benefits of PWYW pricing but keeps price levels less aggressive and more profitable.

CHAPTER 3

Price Context Parameters

Price context parameters surround the focal price and influence its perception. The following seven categories summarize 48 effects on how consumers process information adjacent to a price and how their presence changes consumer preferences and choice:

1. *Anchoring* is a specific psychological phenomenon that this section extends to pricing with multiple studies.
2. *Decoys* summarizes studies on a counterintuitive concept that demonstrates how consumers change their product preferences by introducing an irrelevant choice.
3. *Priming* explains how subtle differences in contextual information can impact consumer behavior on a subconscious level.
4. *Scarcity* gives an overview on the impact of limited availability of a product on product choice.
5. *Product Description* shows how specific cues in product descriptions affect individuals' price perception.
6. *Assortment Presentation* gives an overview on how changes to assortment arrangements affects consumers' willingness to pay.
7. *Sale Tactics* summarize various studies on the way advertisements or sales calls should be organized to improve customers' price acceptance.

Anchoring

Assimilation Anchors

Probably the most cited study exemplifying the anchoring effect was conducted by Tversky and Kahneman (1974): Participants were asked to estimate the percentage of African countries in the United Nations. In the presence of participants, the conductor spun a fortune wheel with numbers between 0 and 100 and asked the participants to first indicate whether the percentage was above or below the number the fortune wheel delivered. Then subjects were instructed to provide their estimate. When participants saw a number of 10 or 65, they estimated percentages of 25 or 45, respectively.

These results showed that people anchored their estimate on an (arbitrary) number and insufficiently adjusted it from there afterwards (Tversky and Kahneman 1974). This insufficient adjustment is the characteristic of assimilation anchors: the anchor attracts the estimate like a magnet.

Applying this concept to pricing, Ariely, Loewenstein, and Prelec (2003) showed participants in an experiment different common products (cordless keyboard, average wine, Belgian chocolates etc.) that they could actually buy. At first, subjects should decide whether they were willing to pay an amount higher or lower than the last two digits of their social security number. Then they stated their maximum willingness to pay for each product. When the researchers compared responses from those students with a social security number in the top 20% to those in the bottom 20% they found the willingness to pay was two times higher for students with a high social security number confirming a strong anchoring effect also in the domain of prices.

In summary, providing a random number influences people's judgment regardless of whether subjects are told this would happen, whether they are paid for accurate estimates or if the anchor is completely off (e.g. "Is the average temperature in San Francisco higher or lower than 558 degrees Fahrenheit (292 degrees Celsius)? What is the average temperature of San Francisco?") (Quattrone et al. 1984; Tversky and Kahneman 1974; Wilson et al. 1996). Given the pervasiveness of the anchoring effect and its long history in various research disciplines, Ariely, Loewenstein, and Prelec (2003, p. 75) call it "an old trick from the experimental psychologists' arsenal."

In the following, we look into how research applied the anchoring effect to pricing practice.

Expose consumers to any high number before they start evaluating prices.

Contrast Anchors

Tonight is DVD night. To properly prepare for a pleasant evening, you rush into a supermarket to buy a pack of chips. You grab a bag and notice that the price is $2.50, which is what you expected to pay. When you pass the aisle with all the other chip brands, you see that prices for chips vary between $0.99 and $2.99. Is your choice a good deal? How would you rate the price for your chips if you observed a price range from $1.99 to $3.99?

Up to now, we understand anchors as assimilation anchors. Assimilation anchors pull the evaluation of an object toward them. The opposite are contrast anchors. Contrast anchors push the evaluation of an object into the opposite direction. Replacing an anchor weight of 100 grams with 300 grams makes a 120-gram weight subjectively appear lighter instead of heavier than the 100-gram weight (Sherif, Taub, and Hovland 1958). The 120 grams would be starkly contrasted to the 300-gram weight instead of assimilated with the 100-gram weight.

Janiszewski and Lichtenstein (1999) showed that lifting the end point of a price range in a product category lets consumers perceive a focal price as less expensive.

Cunha Jr. and Shulman (2011) demonstrated that adding a product to an assortment with lower or higher prices than the focal price could do both, increasing or decreasing the perceived price level of a focal product. This effect depends on whether the added product is framed as assimilation anchor (i.e. as similar to other products) or as contrast anchor (i.e. as different from other products).

Summarizing, adding anchors can actually increase perceived distance as visually demonstrated by the Ebbinghaus illusion below – which of the white circles is larger – the left or the right?

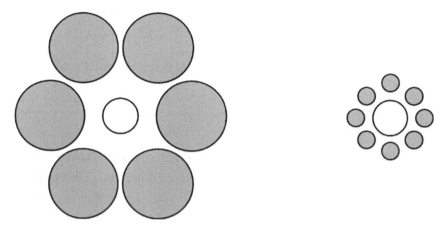

Figure 4: Ebbinghaus illusion

Adding product alternatives at very high price points makes existing products appear less expensive. The same works for adding low-priced items if framed as assimilation anchors.

Suggestive Selling Claims

Would a claim suggesting to buy a certain number of products be effective even when you do not offer a discount?

In an experiment, Wansink, Kent, and Hoch (1998) exposed participants to claims with quantity anchor ("Snickers bar – buy 18 for your freezer") or without anchor ("Snickers bar – buy them for your freezer") and to one of three discount conditions (no discount, 20% or 40% discount). Then subjects indicated their purchase quantity decisions.

Results showed that a quantity anchor had a significant impact on units bought even when no discount was offered. Actually, the relative uplift was largest in the no-discount condition. Purchase quantity went up from 1.4 (without anchor) to 2.6 (with anchor) units – an increase of 86%.

Place selling claims with a quantity anchor. ("Buy 25 Units for Your Freezer!")

Limit per Customer

How do customers react when retailers add the phrase "limit x per customer" to a sale announcement?

Inman, Peter, and Raghubir (1997) found that customers were more willing to buy the promoted product. However, only when the discount was substantial (20% or 50% in the experiment) would customers positively react. When the discount was shallow (5%), this tactic backfired and actually reduced purchase intention compared with the same price discount without restriction. The researchers found that these findings not only hold for purchase limits, but also for time limits ("only available for limited time, expires on...") or purchase preconditions ("only available with a minimum purchase of $x").

However, Wansink, Kent, and Hoch (1998) confirmed the positive impact of purchase limits on demand even when the discount granted was rather modest (soup cans reduced from €0.89 to €0.79, a discount of 12%). The researchers identified an anchoring effect in statements of purchase limits. When the purchase limit was set at four, the average purchase quantity was 3.5. But when the researchers increased the limit to 12 average purchase quantities went up to seven. Comparing to the situation of no limits (73 units sold in total), demand went up by 45% to 106 (limit of four) and by 158% to 188 (limit of 12), respectively.

By the way, as limits subconsciously remind consumers on losses (e.g. miss out opportunities in case of time limits). Consumers are more attuned to promotional messages that are also framed as losses ("save $x") instead of gains ("receive $x") (Choi, Lee, and Ji 2012).

Use purchase limits per customer with high-quantity limits and frame promotional messages as reductions in losses ("Save $x").

Incidental Prices

For any anchor to be effective, do consumers actually need to consciously process the anchoring number?

Adaval and Monroe (2002) showed that anchoring effects also occur even if a random anchor operates below a person's perceptual threshold. Subjects taking part in one experiment exhibited anchoring effects that carried over to another, unrelated study they participated in 48 hours later.

In another experiment, Nunes and Boatwright (2004) set up a makeshift stand to sell a popular CD. Next to the stand, a colleague opened another stand and promoted sweatshirts for sale. There was only one sweatshirt displayed with a price that regularly alternated between $10 and $80. When someone approached the CD stand, the experimenter solicited the person's maximum willingness to pay (applying a somewhat complicated method to avoid under- or overbidding).

The researchers found when the adjacent stand advertised the sweatshirt for $80 people exhibited a higher willingness to pay for the music CD than when a low price of $10 was displayed.

This experiment showed that incidental prices affect consumers' price perception. Incidental prices refer to displayed or paid prices for unrelated products that customers unintentionally encounter.

Put your focal product in the context of higher, unrelated prices.

Precise Anchors

Precise anchors function similarly to precise prices [see section "Price Precision Effect"]. Janiszewski and Uy (2008) found that people tend to adjust to a smaller degree away from precise anchors compared to round anchors.

In their experiments, the researchers asked participants to estimate the sale price of a beach house and provided one of three different anchor values: a list price of $800,000 (rounded anchor), $799,800 (precise under anchor), and $800,200 (precise over anchor).

As expected, respondents provided a significant lower estimate on average for the rounded anchor ($751,867, -6.0%) in comparison to either price version (precise under anchor: $784,671, -1.9%, precise over anchor: $778,264, -2.7%).

Researchers suggest that subjects apply a subjective scale with a finer resolution when exposed to precise anchors. A follow-up analysis on the beach house data showed that rounded anchor values encouraged subjects to provide rounded replies (defined as any multiple of $5,000): When the anchor was rounded, 73% of participants gave a rounded estimate, but only 49% did when the anchor was precise.

When using anchors (e.g. advertised retail price) choose precise numbers.

Product Options and Willingness to Pay

You enter an Italian restaurant and decide on a pizza. The restaurant offers a deluxe pizza with 12 toppings. You can scale it down and save 50 cents per ingredient. How many toppings do you choose? How many would you have chosen if you started with a basic pizza and added toppings to it?

Levin et al. (2002) studied the question whether scaling up a basic product or scaling down a fully loaded uncovers a greater willingness to pay. The researchers hypothesized that downscaling a fully loaded product ends up with more features than when consumers upscale a basic product. The endowment effect should explain this result: Subjects place a greater value on the same product if they possess it compared to if they do not. An anchoring effect might also play a role: Starting with a large number of preselected options might bias consumers toward more finally chosen features.

The researchers asked each of two groups of participants either to scale down a fully loaded pizza with 12 toppings or to scale up a basic pizza. Price of the basic pizza was $5 with each ingredient costing 50 cents so that the starting price of the fully loaded pizza was $11. In the scaling up case, participants would have to pay 50 cents for each added topping whereas subjects assigned to the scaling down case would be credited with 50 cents for each ingredient they left off.

Levin et al. (2002) observed that subjects in the scaling down condition chose on average 5.29 toppings compared with 2.71 in the scaling up condition.

Overall, allowing consumers to downscale a fully loaded deluxe version biases consumers toward a product with more features, eliciting a higher willingness to pay.

If you offer a modular product with multiple, optional features, asking customers to downscale a fully loaded product results in a better-equipped product and greater willingness to pay instead of upgrading a basic product.

Reference Prices: How Customers Evaluate Prices

When you see a price, what is the outcome of your evaluation? Probably, you develop judgments like, this price is "cheap," "reasonable," or "too expensive." How do you come to this conclusion?

Consumers develop an internal reference price (IRP), a standard price against which offered prices are compared (Monroe 1973). This standard price could be the previous price paid, the average market price, or the highest price willing to pay. Lowengart (2002) summarized 26 possible ways people could define their internal reference price.

This internal reference price is not a fixed price point. As we saw in the section "Price Changes," the magnitude of a price change needs to exceed a threshold to be perceived and acted upon. This means consumers maintain a latitude of acceptance so that internal reference prices are understood as a range of acceptable prices. Due to Weber's law, this latitude of acceptance widens in absolute terms as the price increases.

People continuously learn new price information from past purchases, from current offerings of various competitors, from prices of comparable products, from regular or list prices, and so on. When consumers consider this information, they might adjust their internal reference price in either direction (Cheng and Monroe 2013).

Helson's (1964) adaptation level theory explains how existing IRP adapts to a new price information as stimulus. According to Sherif and Hovland's (1961) assimilation-contrast theory, consumers compare new price information with their current IRP and decide whether this new price information is relevant ("assimilate") or too far off ("contrast") to be relevant (e.g. astronomical prices for carpets). Degree of relevance is determined by the relative position (range theory) or ordinal position (range-frequency theory) of new price information between upper and lower bounds of possible price points (Mazumdar, Raj, and Sinha 2005). In other words, consumers might not consider new price information if it is unreasonably high or low.

Marketers seek to raise the customers' IRP. Advertised retail prices (ARPs) function as externally provided price anchors usually with the intention to increase a consumer's IRP (Kalyanaram and Winer 1995). The impact of using ARP as anchors in price promotions is twofold.

On the one hand, Chandrashekaran and Grewal (2006) demonstrate that ARP that exceed IRP raise the latter and adjust it downwards otherwise. Consumers interpret any positive (or negative) difference as a gain (or loss) in line with prospect theory: Gains (losses) increase (decrease) attractiveness of an offer and sale price.

On the other hand, frequent sales and discounts raise doubts about the real price for promoted products putting downward pressure on the IRP (Mazumdar, Raj, and Sinha 2005). Hence, Greenleaf (1995) found that using irregular discounts is the most profitable pricing strategy reducing impact on IRP. With a similar rationale, marketers should explain reasons for a discount so customers are less likely to expect future discounts that would let their IRP drop otherwise (Mazumdar, Raj, and Sinha 2005).

To evaluate a price, consumers compare a focal price to their IRP and map it on a subjective price scale (Monroe 1973). The subjective price scale expresses the relative expensiveness of the price encountered, like "acceptable" or "expensive" that ultimately drives offer evaluation and purchase intentions (see Figure 5). This encoding process explains why consumers cannot recall an exact price but can tell whether the price is acceptable or not (Monroe and Lee 1999).

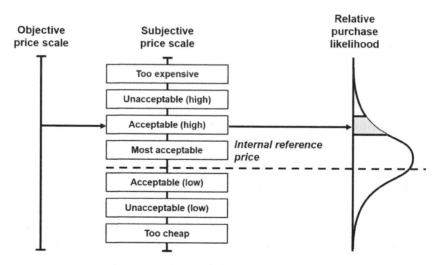

Figure 5: Mapping objective prices on subjective prices
(adapted from Monroe 1973)

Customers maintain an internal standard of comparison against which they evaluate prices. Marketers should aim at increasing the positive difference between the customer's internal reference price and the sale price to foster deal attractiveness.

Exaggerated Reference Prices

You are shopping for a new TV set that you expect to cost about $360. You find it in one store and you are happily surprised that this one is on sale. The advertisement states: "Regular price: $799, today: $319". What do you think – is it a good deal or a bad trick?

The most common and easiest way to provide an external anchor is to display an advertised regular price (ARP). But, does it backfire when your ARP is unreasonably high?

Urbany, Bearden, and Weilbaker (1988) suggest a "discount hypothesis" meaning that although consumers do not believe an exaggerated reference price, they do not reject (i.e. "contrast") but discount it. As the discounting remains insufficient, the researchers found that exaggerated reference prices still exert the same positive impact on deal perception as plausible reference prices – despite lower believability scores for the former. The researchers asked participants in an experiment to evaluate the value of an offer. The design of this experiment ensured that subjects had a similar price expectation of about $360. Results showed when different ARPs were presented ($359, $419, $799) for the same sale price ($319), consumers increased their internal reference price and perceived the value of the highest ARP as highest.

In sum, hard to believe, but consumers believe even unbelievable comparison prices.

Exaggerated comparison prices remain effective despite low believability.

Exaggerated Reference Prices and Time Pressure

Under time pressure, people rationalize and behave differently. Time pressure limits people's cognitive resources, forcing them to refer to simple heuristics to evaluate purchase decisions (Suri and Monroe 2003). As people become less risk averse and less skeptical about messages presented to them, Krishnan, Dutta, and Jha (2013) reasoned that consumers might also be less critical about exaggerated advertised regular prices when they experience time pressure.

In an experiment, researchers presented participants with four versions of the same ad and just changed the slogan ("Weekend Sale," no time pressure vs. "Weekend Sale only," time pressure, and the level of an advertiser's regular price (ARP) (plausible ARP vs. exaggerated ARP).

The exaggerated ARP increased purchase intentions compared to the plausible ARP when time pressure was absent. This finding replicated earlier studies on the impact of exaggerated reference prices (e.g. Urbany, Bearden, and Weilbaker 1988).

When participants experienced time pressure, shopping intentions further increased for exaggerated ARPs (Krishnan, Dutta, and Jha 2013). The research team found the same results when participants were set under "real" time pressure (i.e. participants were told to complete a task in two minutes that would usually require four minutes).

When displaying exaggerated advertised retail prices (ARP), introduce cues to solicit feeling of time pressure.

Decoys

Product Decoy Effect

A product decoy is the answer to a less obvious question: How does the addition of an irrelevant brand to an existing set influence your brand choice?

Given that this product is irrelevant and is not expected to attract a sales share greater than 2%, why should this offer affect your purchase decision by its pure presence?

The following effects explain why and how you can manipulate the preferences of your customers toward a target brand by adding an additional product – the product decoy.

Decoy products are a means to influence brand preferences of consumers in favor of a target product, which is not the decoy.

Attraction Effect or Asymmetrical Domination

Ariely (2010) took the following advertisement from *The Economist*: Internet subscription to Economist.com for $59 and print-and-Internet subscription for $125. Which subscription would you prefer? How would your decision change if a third option was introduced: *Internet subscription for $59, print-only subscription for $125 or print-and-Internet subscription for $125?*

Ariely (2010) tested both versions in an experiment. When only two options were available Ariely showed that 68% of participants would choose the Internet subscription while 32% would subscribe to the print-and-Internet version. However, when the third option was introduced, 84% would choose the print-and-Internet subscription, 16% would select the internet subscription and 0% would opt for the print-only version. Why does the introduction of a third, irrelevant option nobody chose impact consumer choice when remaining options did not change?

Huber, Payne, and Puto (1982) showed that the addition of an asymmetrically dominated option increases the attractiveness of the existing option that is dominating (target brand). The added decoy brand does not attract much demand but shifts consumer choice away from the competitor brand to the target brand. This is why this effect is usually referred to as attraction effect. Assuming there are two products on the market to which a third option (decoy) is added with following characteristics:

	Price	Quality rating
Target brand	$2.00	50
Competitor brand	$2.50	70
Decoy	$2.20	30

The target brand and the competitor brand do not dominate each other on both performance dimensions. This means no brand is clearly better than the other in terms of pricing and quality, so that choosing one option becomes a trade-off: The target brand is less expensive but with lower quality ratings than the competitor brand. The decoy is more expensive than the target brand but cheaper than the competing brand. In terms of quality, the decoy is dominated by both existing brands. This example illustrates what "asymmetrically dominated" means: the decoy is only dominated by the target brand, but not the other brand.

In their experiment, Huber, Payne, and Puto (1982) provided similar information as shown in the table above and asked participants which brands they would choose. In the first round, the researchers exposed subjects to a choice set including the decoy, but removed the decoy when they asked participants again two weeks later.

Results revealed that on average, the decoy increased choice share of target brand by nine percentage points relative to a base share without decoy of 50% equaling to a relative shift in demand of 18%.

Why does the decoy happen at all? If consumers do not have strong preferences for either of both attributes (price vs. quality rating) of the initial brands, they become indifferent to both options. In this situation a third, clearly dominated option breaks the tie and provides an opportunity to convincingly justify a purchase of the dominating brand (Simonson 1989).

> *When customers are indifferent to two brands, adding an asymmetrically dominated option attracts customers toward the (dominating) target brand.*

Attraction Effect with Weak Decoys

Does the decoy effect also work when the decoy is not fully dominated but slightly better than the target brand in one dimension – which might be a more realistic scenario in the marketplace?

Huber and Puto (1983) explain that as long as the decoy offers a relatively unattractive trade-off – for example just a 3% lower price for a 20% decrease in quality – the decoy effect still works. The researchers refer to this decoy as "weak decoy."

Just to remember, a (weak) decoy attracts demand away from the competitor brand. If the weak decoy becomes stronger, it does not equally attract demand from both existing brands but rather from the more similar brand – also known as similarity hypothesis (Tversky 1972). When Huber and Puto (1983) replaced a weak decoy with a strong version choice, share of the target brand dropped from 60% to 51% while the decoy's share increased from 7% to 15%, the competitor's share remained at 33% (difference from 100% is due to rounding errors).

Weak product decoys still work as long as they do not become strong.

> *An effective product decoy does not need to be fully dominated by the target brand: an unattractive trade-off is sufficient.*

When the Attraction Effect Works Best

The attraction effect or asymmetrically dominated effect require a few conditions to be effective. After more than 30 years since they discovered the underlying effects, Huber, Payne, and Puto (2014) propose following requirements for an attraction effect to unfold:

- Consumers are unsure about their trade-off evaluations. Is an additional half-a-star in customer rating worth a 20% higher price?

- Similarly, consumers have relatively weak or uninformed preferences between target and competitor, so a decoy can effectively change their preference order.

- Consumers can easily identify the asymmetrical dominance relationship. Which product dominates which other product? Presentation is crucial, which means target brand and decoy are physically close to one another and product attributes are expressed as values so that people can effortlessly evaluate both brands.

- The decoy is attractive to the consumer. If the decoy is unattractive per se and the dominance relationship does not provide any value to the decider, then an attraction effect is unlikely to play out.

- If the decoy is viable and too strong, an additional, irrelevant product can hardly influence the decision and an attraction effect might not occur.

In addition, Heath and Chatterjee (1995) showed that decoys are more effective if they target high-priced/high-quality brands instead of low-priced/low-quality products. A decoy that is dominated by the low-priced/low-quality product might be regarded as undesired so that its domination does not provide any value to the consumer.

Doyle et al. (1999) ran a field study in a supermarket and confirmed this conclusion. The researchers chose as core brand the high-priced/high-quality (HPHQ) product Heinz baked beans and as a low-priced/low-quality (LPLQ) alternative the retail store's own brand, "VG baked beans." As an HPHQ decoy, the researchers decided on the same Heinz baked beans but at a higher price. As an LPLQ decoy, they opted for damaged tins of a third brand that was already perceived as inferior to VG baked beans.

Results from this experiment showed that demand for Heinz baked beans increased from a choice share of 65% to 76% when the HPHQ decoy was present (decoy share: 12%). However, when the LPLQ decoy was used, target brand VG baked beans did not attract significantly more demand.

> *Product decoys work best when (a) consumers have no strong opinion about product alternatives, (b) consumers actually identify the dominance relationship between products, (c) the decoy is designed as a "weak" option, and (d) decoy products target high-priced/high-quality brands.*

Compromise Effect

Research so far covered fully dominated product decoys and more competitive but still weak decoys with an unattractive trade-off in product features. Can a viable option still shift demand toward a target brand?

As customers are risk averse and avoid extreme options, they tend to choose the middle, the compromise option (Simonson 1989; Simonson and Tversky 1992). This compromise effect is particularly strong when consumers feel a need to justify their purchases to an imaginary or real third person and when they are unclear about this third person's preferences. The middle option can be justified the easiest as experiments and think-aloud protocols showed (Simonson 1989).

In one experiment, Simonson and Tversky (1992) offered two cameras to participants: a Minolta X-370 for $169.99 and the Minolta Maxxum 3000i for $239.99. Choice shares for both cameras were equal at 50%.

When the researchers introduced a third, upscale option – Minolta Maxxum 7000i for $469.99 – share for the low-scale option fell to 22% whereas the middle option increased to 57%. The relative preference rose from 50% (= 50% / (50% +50%)) to 72% (= 57% / (22% + 57%)). Simonson (1989) conducted a couple of experiments covering various product categories – from mouthwash to television to apartments. Results revealed that on average choice share increased by 17.5% when a product became the compromise option.

Kim (2017) investigated factors that could strengthen or weaken the compromise effect. The researcher assumed that the more salient the relative performance of each option is to the consumer, the stronger the compromise effect becomes. Hence, he looked into the effect of presenting the trade-off between available options either numerically (as a table) or graphically (as a two-dimensional graph). In various experiments, the researcher found that the compromise effect did not exist when the trade-off was presented numerically, but it was significant when the presentation was graphical. This effect was more profound when subjects had to make the choice decision under time pressure.

In summary, introducing a third, extreme option shifts consumers' preferences to the middle option.

> *Introduce an extreme option: When consumers feel the need to justify their purchase to themselves or (imaginary) others and are unclear about their own preferences, they tend to choose the middle option. This effect is more profound when the middle option is graphically presented as such and when consumers choose under time pressure.*

Attribute Decoy Effect

Suppose you are shopping for a down jacket. You reduced your choice set to two alternatives. Both have the same fill ratings, the same cover material, the same stitching and have the same price. However, they differ in filling: one jacket has "regular down filling" the other "alpine class fill." Which one would you buy? If someone revealed that "alpine class" does not make a difference would you change your choice?

Carpenter, Glazer, and Nakamoto (1994) studied these questions and found that consumers preferred those brands that had added an irrelevant attribute. This preference did not diminish when its irrelevance was revealed and subjects even acknowledged there was no difference between "alpine class fill" and "regular fill." Communication theory suggests that consumers infer that an irrelevant attribute might still have a meaning and provide value.

However, the researchers found that this impact differs by price level (low, high, premium). If the price level was low – relative to alternative brands – adding an irrelevant attribute did not impact brand evaluation at all. If the price level was at a premium level in comparison to competitors, an irrelevant attribute raised brand evaluation but dropped back when its irrelevance was revealed. However, for relatively high prices an additional, irrelevant attribute improved brand valuation even if its irrelevance was revealed.

Researchers suggested the distinctiveness justifying higher prices stems from this additional attribute. Revelation that the distinctive attribute is irrelevant does not seem to reduce the consumers' inference.

Consumers find justification for (reasonably) higher prices in irrelevant attributes.

Priming

Background Symbols in Online Environment

How do "atmospherics" in an online context influence customers' purchase decisions? Would you agree that your preference for a product changes with different background symbols that you see on a website?

A subtle information, a cue, can activate a specific bit of information in memory. Once activated, people can more easily access this piece of information so that it receives more weight in decision tasks (Yi 1990).

More importantly, this process – called priming – usually functions subconsciously so that individuals are not aware of it happening, and when educated about priming, people doubt that it would affect them (Herr 1989).

Mandel and Johnson (2002) demonstrate the effectiveness of priming in an online context. The researchers asked participants in an experiment to choose between two offered products. As products, the researchers selected cars and sofas. First, participants chose between a less safe, but cheaper car and a safer, but more expensive alternative. Second, subjects selected either a less comfortable and less expensive sofa or a costlier and more comfortable option.

The researchers constructed different versions of background for otherwise identical websites. Each product choice was preceded by a welcome page. The background of the welcome page prior to the car choice was in red/orange color and contained flames (prime for safety) or was colored in green showing dollar bills (prime for price). The background of the second welcome page introducing the sofa choice was either colored in blue with clouds (prime for comfort) or in green with pennies (prime for price).

Results showed that the choice share for the cheaper car was 65.8% when subjects were primed on price and 50% when subjects saw the safety prime. Likewise, 55.8% of participants who were primed on price chose the cheaper sofa, but only 38.7% when exposed to the comfort prime.

This experiment demonstrated that website design can actually influence consumer choice within the same set of products and product descriptions.

Exposure to the right primes (money vs. benefit) can influence consumers to purchase more or less expensive product alternatives.

Time versus Money Effect

When buying a product, do you want to think about the benefits of its consumption or the money to be paid? How could you provide subtle cues to nudge customers to think about consumption instead of money?

Mogilner and Aaker (2009) developed the following theory about the impact of reminding consumers on time instead of money aspects in buying situations: When people feel personally connected to a product, they develop more positive attitudes toward the product, which translates ultimately in greater value perception and willingness to pay. Making the concept of "time" salient to consumers causes them to think about the experience of product consumption, which in turn strengthens their personal connection with the product. The concept of "money" does not have the same impact – it is "a colder unit of exchange" that rather personally disconnects consumers when activated.

To test this theory, Mogilner and Aaker (2009) opened a lemonade stand in a park in San Francisco. They put up a sign stating "Spend a little time, and enjoy C & D's lemonade" to activate the concept of time; "Spend a little money, and enjoy C & D's lemonade" to activate money; or "Enjoy C & D's lemonade" to activate neither. The sign alternated every 10 minutes to randomize exposure to passersby. When people stopped at the stand, they were asked to pay any amount between $1 and $3 for a glass of lemonade. After their purchase, customers filled a short satisfaction survey.

Results from this experiment showed that in the time condition, the share of passersby who bought a glass of lemonade (14%) was twice the share in the money condition (7%). For the control condition, the share was 9%. In terms of willingness to pay, customers who were nudged toward time paid on average 81% ($2.50) more than customers seeing the money sign ($1.38). Customers in the control condition paid on average $2.18. In line with the theoretical reasoning, "time" consumers also gave more favorable attitude ratings toward the product than did consumers in the money or control group.

In a purchase situation, draw consumers' attention to time rather than money criteria.

Color of (Online/Offline) Environment

Have you noticed how different colors influence your mood and decision making?

As psychological studies have documented that red color induces aggression, Bagchi and Cheema (2013) reasoned that consumers would exhibit a different willingness to pay depending on the selling mechanism, i.e. auction-type or negotiation-type. Studies usually contrast red to blue as the latter is associated with cool and calm. In auction-type selling situations, aggressive buyers focus on beating other bidders and are willing to pay higher prices. In negotiation settings, aggressive buyers concentrate on getting a good deal and make lower offers. In the context of eBay auctions, the researchers confirmed that a red background induced more aggressive bidding behavior (higher bid jumps) and an overall higher willingness to pay. Conversely, for negotiations, the research showed that consumers exposed to red made lower offers and exhibited a lower willingness to pay.

In the context of offline shopping situations when consumers browse around as part of their buying process, a blue colored retail interior makes consumers feel more comfortable, decreases purchase postponement, and lifts their likelihood to purchase relative to red (Bellizzi and Hite 1992).

Babin, Hardesty, and Suter (2003) compared the impact of lighting on blue- and orange-colored interiors. When soft lights were used, consumers expressed similar purchase intentions for orange and blue colored conditions. But when bright lights were used, consumers were more willing to buy in a blue-colored environment and less likely to purchase when the interior was colored orange.

> *In online auction-settings, red increases willingness to pay, but it reduces when red is used in (online) negotiation situations. In an offline purchase context, blue makes customers feel more comfortable in shopping situations and more willing to buy. If your store interior has the wrong color, use soft lights.*

Small Words Effect

How do words change perception of prices although these words refer to something else than prices?

In previous sections, we saw that the congruency effect is effective when magnitude differences are visually presented (font size, spatial separation). This effect is more subtle. Research suggests that a dimension that is less relevant to the displayed price but is semantically related to magnitude per se could still exert an impact on magnitude perception (Sharma and McKenna 1998). This effect is called "semantic gradient effect." In a classic experiment, Klein (1964) demonstrated that participants whose task was to name the color of a word needed more time when the word was semantically more closely related to the ink's color (e.g. "fire" written in red).

Coulter and Coulter (2005) presented participants in an experiment with advertisements showing a regular price and a lower sale price in the same font size. As semantic cues, the researchers added short tag lines referring to product performance – either "low friction" (congruent condition) or "high performance" (incongruent condition) – next to the lower sale price. As a result, customers perceived prices as better (though not statistically significant) and were more likely (this time statistically significant) to buy the product when a word related to smallness ("<u>low</u> friction") was added in proximity to the smaller sale price.

Add words related to the semantic magnitude category you want a target number to associate with (e.g. "low" for prices or "high" for discounts).

Scarcity

Scarcity and Future Discounts

You are about to buy a pair of jeans in a department store. Fortunately, you find that your favorite brand is on sale next week at a 10% discount. Looking for your size, you observe that only two pairs are left. Do you buy your pair of jeans today or wait until next week? How would decide if 10 pairs were left or the discount was 50% off?

Gabler and Reynolds (2013) conducted an experiment and asked participants whether they would buy a pair of jeans today or wait until next week when these jeans would be offered at a discount. In their scenario descriptions, the researchers changed the level of scarcity (low: "two pairs left" vs. high: "10 pairs left") and level of future discount (low: 10% off, moderate: 25% off, high: 50% off).

Results showed on average that subjects were 34% more likely to buy today when scarcity was high compared to low. In addition, with each increase in future discount level (i.e. from 10% to 25% off, and from 25% to 50% off), people were 26% more likely to postpone their purchases: the experiment demonstrated that participants were 26% more likely to buy next week instead of today at "25% off" versus "10% off" and an additional 26% more likely to postpone at "50% off" versus "25% off."

However, diving deep on the results revealed that a low future discount indeed increased purchase likelihood at full price even in the low scarcity condition. The researchers also discovered this finding when the product was scarce, but showed that a higher, moderate future discount further increased purchase likelihood at full price today.

In sum, when retailers have to clear their stock to accommodate new inventory, they can optimize full-price sales with the right scarcity/future discount condition.

To maximize sales at full price, combine a scarcity cue with a future discount.

Scarcity, Product Involvement and Price Level

Imagine you are about to buy a CD of the very first concert of your favorite music band. You find the CD at the flea market – only one copy is available. How excited are you? And how much were you willing to pay? How would you feel if three items were offered?

Gabler and Reynolds (2013) found that scarcity itself provides an emotional value to consumers that are highly involved in comparison to low-involvement customers. The researchers conducted an experiment in the context of a flea market. Participants were asked about the maximum price they were willing to pay for a CD of their favorite music artist or band (average response: $23). Then the researchers exposed subjects to one of two scenarios. In the low-scarcity case, three CDs were available and in the high-scarcity case only one. Then participants were asked whether they would prefer to buy immediately the CD at a price $5 above their maximum price or wait until the next Saturday when all unsold items would be offered at half-price. Additional questions captured the subjects' level of involvement with the product.

Results revealed no statistical difference on purchase likelihood for low-involvement individuals depending on level of scarcity (low scarcity: 53% vs. high scarcity: 61%). But for high-involvement individuals, their willingness to buy increased from 53% to 85% when scarcity changed from low to high. Notably, 85% would prefer to buy immediately at a price that was actually 22% ($5/$23) higher than their reservation price when the product was scarce. Hence, the researchers discovered that high-involvement customers place more weight on scarcity in their purchase decisions, whereas low-involvement customers consider future discounts.

When the product category shifted to clothing (i.e. a pair of jeans) in a retail context, these results reversed. Following up on the study introduced above [see section "Scarcity and Future Discount"], the researchers analyzed the dataset separately for low-involvement and high-involvement customers.

They found that participants with low involvement made their decisions based on the level of scarcity, while high-involvement customers considered level of future discounts: Low involvement customers were 56% more likely to purchase a product when scarcity was high. The level of discounts did not (statistically significantly) affect their decision. For highly involved individuals, their purchase likelihood decreased by 35% with each discount stage tested in the experiment – i.e. from low (10% off) to moderate (25% off) and from moderate to high (50% off). The level of scarcity had no effect on their purchase likelihood.

Why do highly involved customers consider only the level of future discounts? The researchers reasoned that those customers are product experts and are well aware of the product's usual price, which might explain those individuals' price consciousness. Low-involvement customers are less knowledgeable about a product and conclude a better quality from higher prices. Thus, low-involvement customers are more inclined to buy when the product's availability is made salient compared to future higher discounts.

In sum, whether scarcity provides an additional, emotional value, combined with the level of customer involvement, explain how scarcity and future discounts affect people's likelihood to purchase.

Similarly, Suri, Kohli, and Monroe (2007) found that scarcity cues were most effective for low-priced products when customers exhibit low involvement and for high-priced products when customers were highly involved. Scarcity stresses perception of a low price in the former case and underscores a high quality in the latter case. For opposite combinations (low price/high involvement; high price/low involvement) scarcity decreases value perceptions and purchase intentions.

To decide about an optimal scarcity cue or scarcity cue / future discount combination, you need to consider the customer's product involvement, the emotional value attached to scarcity and the product's price.

Scarcity during Market Introduction

You are excited; the new Tesla model will be introduced in your region in the upcoming month. Elon Musk promises that everyone who wants to drive the new Tesla will get one. How does this promise affect you purchase likelihood? Would your propensity to order change if Elon Musk had announced that only 5,000 cars will be made available this year?

When a specialty product – in contrast to commodity products – is introduced to a market, consumers are uncertain about the product's quality. One way to signal a high level of quality to potential customers and to raise prospects' willingness to pay is to reduce supply (Stock and Balachander 2005).

Balachander, Liu, and Stock (2009) analyzed the U.S. passenger car market with six years of sale, inventory, and price data for about 140 models in a given year.

The researchers found that car manufacturers introducing new models with scarcity to the market actually increased sales (after accounting for forgone sales). More precisely, a reduction of inventory of 1% relative to the industry average increased market share by an average of 0.46% for new cars.

When introducing specialty products to a new market, limit supply.

Scarcity and Conspicuous Products

You are an Apple fan – not to say an Apple enthusiastic and Apple evangelist. The new iPhone model is introduced and immediately added to your must-have list. In terms of color, you are more or less indifferent. When you enter the Apple store, you read below the black version "due to limited supply, only five units available" and below the white version "due to high demand, nearly sold out." Which color do you choose?

With the consumption of conspicuous products (e.g. mobile phone, wristwatch, laptop) people want to express uniqueness and belonging to special groups. Gierl and Huettl (2010) concluded that buyers of conspicuous products are more likely to be attracted by scarcity due to limited supply ("limited edition," "due to limited supply, only x units available in the U.S.") compared to scarcity due to demand ("due to high demand, nearly sold out").

The researchers confirmed that statements about supply-side scarcity improved attractiveness of conspicuous products. Claims about demand-side scarcity actually reduced product evaluation ratings for conspicuous products compared to the situation without any scarcity cues.

To promote conspicuous products, add claims on limited supply.

Scarcity and Non-Conspicuous Products

You ran out of shampoo, which, in turn, makes you run to the nearest supermarket. As you do not have a favorite brand, you look around and find the following messages. For brand A you read, "Due to limited supply, only 10 units available" and for brand B you see "due to high demand, nearly sold out." Which shampoo brand do you choose?

When buyers evaluate commodity, non-conspicuous products (e.g. shampoo, flash light, chocolate bar) they conclude better quality from higher demand. For those products, Gierl and Huettl (2010) reasoned that demand-induced scarcity cues ("due to high demand, only x units left") are more effective in signaling a higher level of demand than supply-side scarcity claims. The researchers indeed found that demand-side scarcity claims raised perceived attractiveness for non-conspicuous products. The results reversed for supply-side scarcity cues.

Verhallen and Robben (1994) tested the impact of scarcity on consumer preferences for a product (a recipe book) that could be classified as either a non-conspicuous or conspicuous product in an experiment. They found that limited availability due to high demand and due to limited supply independently improved preference ratings so that participants gave highest ratings when both scarcity cues were present – i.e. limited edition due to high demand – nearly sold out.

To promote commodity products, add claims on limited availability due to excessive demand. If products cannot be clearly defined as either commodity or specialty products, scarcity cues due to limited supply and excessive demand combined might increase demand.

Product Description

Price Primacy Effect

Does it matter whether customers are exposed to a price tag first instead of the product and its features?

Karmarkar, Shiv, and Knutson (2015) investigated this question and invited participants to enter a neural scanner. Before climbing into the scanner, researchers gave each participant $40 to spend at their disposal for products they would be shown during the experiment. While in the brain scanner, participants saw various products and corresponding prices in varying order (price first or product first) and were asked about their willingness to spend from their budget of $40.

Results confirmed a different pattern of brain activity in the price primacy versus the product primacy condition suggesting that price primacy increases the importance of a product's monetary worth relative to the product's desirability. Changing the primacy condition from product to price suggests that customers also change their criterion for purchases from "Do I like it?" to "Is it worth it?" (Karmarkar, Shiv, and Knutson 2015, p. 476).

The study revealed that participants purchased more utilitarian products and regarded these products as more worthy when price was shown first.

Based on these findings, the researchers recommend marketers present prices first if the product is utilitarian and the price is a real bargain and not a misleading promotion.

Reveal prices before presenting the product if the product is utilitarian and price is an actual bargain.

Mental Accounting and Self-Control

Consumers set up mental accounts to track, manage, and evaluate their financial activities. Thaler (1985, p. 199) illustrates the way mental accounts function with the following example: "Mr. and Mrs. J have saved $15,000 toward their dream vacation home. They hope to buy the home in five years. The money earns 10% in a money market account. They just bought a new car for $11,000, which they financed with a three-year car loan at 15%."

Economically, family J would have been better off if they had taken the money to buy the car from their account instead of financing it. But they set up two separate accounts, a "vacation home" account and a "car" account. Amounts are not transferrable between these accounts.

Why do consumers set up mental accounts in the first place? Consumers want to keep track of their financial expenses, judge expected and actual outcomes of their financial decisions, and control their spending behavior with efficient use of time and mental effort (Thaler 1999).

How do consumers evaluate mental accounts? Outcomes of financial transactions are evaluated following the value function described in prospect theory by Tversky and Kahneman (1974). That is, outcomes are coded as gains or losses, which in turn are evaluated following the rules of hedonic framing (integrating, segregating). [See also section "Prospect Theory and Value Function."]

If a mental account is expected to close in black – i.e. all gains and losses lead to an overall positive value – consumers will likely engage in a transaction.

Consumers keep separate mental accounts to track, evaluate and control financial transactions and spending behavior.

Mental Accounting and Ambiguous Framing

To control spending behavior, consumers divide expenses into different mental accounts and assign budgets to each account (Heath and

Soll 1996). When consumers face a new transaction, they need to decide to which account they would assign associated expenses.

Cheema and Soman (2006) found that consumers have degrees of freedom to assign an expense to different accounts, and they would use this ambiguity to justify their expenses. The researchers showed that participants in an experiment would assign a dinner to either a "food" or "entertainment" account depending on which mental account left a surplus to accommodate this expense.

When describing a product, provide a broad range of benefits and frame it ambiguously to help customers find a mental account that could justify this expense.

Transaction Utility: Value beyond Product Benefit

In an apparel store, you find a pair of boots on sale for $69 instead of regular $129. You know you have a reasonable number of boots in your closet and the maximum price you are willing to pay for another pair of boots is $50. But you buy the boots anyway. Why?

Thaler (1985) proposed that consumers evaluate two parts of a transaction independently: acquisition utility and transaction utility.

Acquisition utility refers to the loss or gain a consumer associates with the purchase of the product itself. It represents the maximum price a customer is willing to pay (also known as reservation price) minus the actual price paid. Economists refer to this difference as consumer surplus.

Transaction utility refers to the value gained from a transaction itself. It corresponds to the difference between the internal reference price a consumer believes is fair for the given product and the actual price itself.

Applied to the introductory example, the acquisition utility is negative while the transaction utility is positive. The overall evaluation results in a positive value that led to the purchase decision.

Thaler (1985) explained the concept with this classic example:

"You are lying on the beach on a hot day. All you have to drink is ice water. For the last hour, you have been thinking about how much you would enjoy a nice cold bottle of your favorite brand of beer. A companion gets up to go make a phone call and offers to bring back a beer from the only nearby place where beer is sold (a fancy resort hotel) [a small, run-down grocery store]. He says that the beer might be expensive and so asks how much you are willing to pay for the beer. He says that he will buy the beer if it costs as much or less than the price you state. But if it costs more than the price you state he will not buy it. You trust your friend, and there is no possibility of bargaining with (the bartender) [storeowner]. What price do you tell him?"

In the case of a fancy resort, subjects were willing to pay $2.65, and in the grocery store case, $1.50. Acquisition utility is the same in both cases as you drink the same beer at the beach and do not consume any pleasant atmosphere from the fancy resort. The difference is explained by transaction utility. You expect a higher price at the fancy resort so that your internal reference price increases accordingly and allows a higher actual price that delivers the same value as in the grocery store case.

In summary, the context of a transaction influences consumers' willingness to pay, despite the same value derived from the focal product.

Create the right context to provide additional value beyond benefits derived from the core product.

Country Image Effect

You are about to get a new pair of sport shoes. Usually you buy Nikes – but this time you think about giving the less popular brand Brooks a try. You learned that they manufacture their shoes in the U.S. How much would you consider spending on a pair of Brooks'? The next day you read about Brooks' plans of moving their plants to South Korea – how does this news affect your willingness to pay?

Koschate-Fischer, Diamantopoulos, and Oldenkotte (2012) reasoned that a positive country image adds to brand equity, which in turn leads to a higher willingness to pay if a brand is associated with a country holding a positive image.

After confirming that France has a more favorable country image than Austria, the researchers let participants reveal their willingness to pay for a brand producing their mineral water in France or Austria, respectively. The experiment showed that consumers would spend about a third more when the brand produced its products in a country with a more favorable country image (France: €1.02 vs. Austria: €0.77). By the way, brand familiarity with the French or Austrian brand did not impact the subjects' willingness to pay so that any difference was attributable solely to country image.

In a high-involvement context, the researchers asked participants to imagine they were about to buy sport shoes. In this experiment, subjects were exposed to sport shoes that differed in brand familiarity (high: Nike, low: Brooks) and were produced in countries with different images (favorable country image: U.S., less favorable country image: South Korea). Results showed when either brand was produced in the U.S., willingness to pay was statistically identical. However, when subjects learned that the low-familiarity brand was produced in South Korea, willingness to pay dropped by 18% (from $81.51 to $61.59) whereas for the high-familiarity brand, consumers' willingness to pay did not change.

These results suggest that companies producing in a country with a favorable image should emphasize their country-of-origin in their marketing communication. Furthermore, low familiar brands should think twice about moving their production facilities to a country with a less favorable image to save costs. Actually, if a low-familiar brand is currently producing in such a country, they could consider moving their production to a country with a more favorable image to improve their pricing position. The latter holds for low-involvement products in particular.

In addition, Hu and Wang (2010) found that the home country image of a retailer – instead of the producer's – also improves consumers' willingness to pay. Based on eBay transactions, their research showed that buyers were willing to pay more for the same product when the seller was located in a country with a more favorable country image.

Producing in (or selling from) a country with a favorable image increases consumers' willingness to pay, in particular for low-involvement products or unfamiliar brands.

Assortment Presentation

Product Order by Brand

As the new head of electronics products of a local store, you are wondering about changing the presentation of your products. Should you order them by brand – or by price?

Would you decide differently if you joined a discount store chain and were thinking about sorting low-priced products?

Suri et al. (2012) presented 21 DVD players sorted either by brand (A to Z) or by price (ascending order) to participants in an experiment and asked them to evaluate price and quality perception of two target products, a high-priced brand and a low-priced alternative.

The researchers found that, when products were sorted by brand, consumers gave high-priced targets higher ratings on perceived quality and overall value and lower ratings on perceived sacrifice. However, when products were sorted by price, results were reversed. For low-priced target products, consumers evaluated perceived quality and overall value as higher and perceived sacrifice as lower.

The studies also revealed that sorting by prices makes consumers look for alternative brands and spend more time with product evaluations. In case of price sorts, the concept of price becomes more salient, which is beneficial for low-priced products but hurts quality of perception for high-priced products.

However, these findings hold only if consumers sought to buy a product. If subjects only browsed through the assortment, the way of sorting had no impact on perception of quality, price, or value.

This research recommends that retailers with relatively high prices sort alternatives by brand to enhance quality perception. Sorting by price is more suitable for retailers who offer low prices or frequent sale promotions.

Sorting by brand improves value perception for retailers offering high-priced alternatives whereas price sorts are more advantageous for retailers with relatively low prices.

Product Order by Price

When designing a menu, if you decide to organize it by prices, what is the ideal order? Should you sort prices in increasing or decreasing order?

Suk, Lee, and Lichtenstein (2012) suggested that consumers anchor on the first item of the list. As consumers conclude a higher quality from higher prices [see section on Price-Quality Inference] moving down the list consumers have to decide on a trade-off. If prices are sorted in ascending order consumers perceive a loss in prices and a gain in quality; the opposite holds if prices are sorted in descending order. As losses loom larger than gains [see section on Prospect Theory and Value Function] people have a tendency to remain at the top of the list. The researchers conducted an experiment in a local pub serving bottled beer from thirteen brands. Over the course of eight weeks, they would present customers with either an ascending or descending sorted beer menu in every other week.

Results from this experiment confirmed that customers were willing to spend 4.2% more per bottle when prices were listed in descending order.

But Suk, Lee, and Lichtenstein (2012) also found in additional experiments when customers had sufficient product knowledge and could gauge the quality of the respective products without external cues this price order effect diminished.

Sort prices on menus and price lists in descending order.

Product Order by Valence

When you present two product alternatives to your client, should you show your target option first or last?

Krishnamurthy and Nagpal (2010) looked into this question and unearthed the following insight in an experiment.

When presenting positively connoted, attractive products, consumers tend to choose the first, the opposite holds for negatively connoted, not pleasing products (e.g. insurance).

If you are selling a pleasant product (i.e. not insurance) present the target option first otherwise last.

Product Order by Comparison Tactic

Again, you present two products and decide that you stress the target product's relative advantages compared to the other product. Should you present the target product first or second?

Krishnamurthy and Nagpal (2010) found that the frame of comparison (positive versus negative) impacts consumers' preferences for the products presented first and second. Based on their findings we can draw following recommendations:

- If you want to stress relative *advantages* between products (e.g. own vs. competitor) present your product's advantages first, competitor's second and ask which alternative *to reject*.

- In case relative *disadvantages* should be accentuated, present the competitive offer first, your product second and ask which option *to choose*.

Depending on sales tactic – focus on relative advantages or disadvantages of product alternatives – you can influence your customer's choice with the right order of presentation.

Product Order by Sequence

If you were stocking products on shelves, would you place more expensive products to the left or to the right?

People learned that numbers increase from left to the right – for examples on rulers, tape measures, thermometers or two-dimensional graphs – so that consumers associate relative position with magnitude. Following this reasoning, Cai, Shen, and Hui (2012) studied whether consumers would expect higher prices for products presented on the right than on the left. In multiple experiments, the researchers confirmed that consumers evaluated products on the right at higher prices.

Moving from a spatial to a time-wise sequence the researchers also found when products on the right-hand side were presented first to consumers the effect reversed. This finding suggests that people associate higher values not only with location but also with timewise order.

Cai, Shen, and Hui (2012) reasoned as people usually count in ascending order they might spontaneously give a higher estimate for products they process later.

Overall, a number-location and number-order effect might explain these findings.

If you aim at increasing customers' estimates of a product's price, place it on the right-hand side or present it last.

Assortment Density Effect

When you decide for a product and think about how much to pay for it, does it matter whether your product is surrounded by 8 or 25 alternatives?

Bertini, Wathieu, and Iyengar (2012) set up the following experiment. The researchers let participants imagine they were about to buy a white wine for a dinner party and were asked from which price tier they would usually buy from (i.e. cheap, average, expensive). Then the researchers presented pictures of wines from the respective price tier and solicited the maximum willingness to pay for any wine from the presented assortment. As only 3 subjects indicated to buy expensive wines those were excluded from further analysis.

Participants were randomly presented an assortment of 9 or 26 wines sorted in ascending order of quality rating. The lowest and highest ranked wine was kept the same in both conditions so that additional alternatives increased "density" of the assortment without changing the end points of the selection.

Researchers found that consumers who looked for cheap white wines expressed a significant lower willingness to pay when the assortment was dense (26 alternatives) compared to sparse (9 alternatives): $WTP_D = \$8.87$ vs. $WTP_S = \$14.08$, -37%.

For consumers buying an average-priced wine the results reversed. They were willing to spend a higher amount for wine when the assortment was dense instead of sparse: $WTP_D = \$23.56$ vs. $WTP_S = \$17.89$, +32%.

To increase willingness to pay, keep your selection sparse for low-priced products, but offer a broad selection for high-priced products.

Sales Tactics

Sale Sign Effect

When you see that a product is on sale, do you question whether it is indeed a good deal?

Research has repeatedly shown that the mere display of a sale sign encourages sales (Anderson and Simester 2003; Inman, McAlister, and Hoyer 1990). Thus, mixing promotions with negligible discounts with substantial price discounts maximizes profitability (Inman and McAlister 1993). More sale signs drive sales up to a point when about 25% of all products in a category carry a promotional cue (Anderson and Simester 2001). In another study, Anderson and Simester (2003) also looked into the interplay of odd prices and sale signs on demand. They found that a sale cue without a price ending in nine had a stronger impact on demand than a price ending in nine, with or without an "on sale" claim.

When deciding on a sale price accompanied with a sale marker, consider using a price not ending in nine.

The mere display of a "on sale" sign increases purchase likelihood. When marking a price "on sale" use a sale price not ending in nine.

Odd Pricing: Frame of Promotional Messages

Imagine you are about to sign up for a gym membership for $39 per month. You see two different copy texts: "Don't miss out on buying your six-pack from us!" and "Buy your six-pack from us!" Which one resonates better with you?

Schindler and Kirby (1997) suggest that consumers perceive nine-ending price as a round amount and a small gain. Following this rationale that people infer gains from odd pricing, Choi, Lee, and Ji (2012) conclude consumers are more easily influenced by promotional messages that are framed as gains ("gain $x") instead off reduction in losses ("save $x").

The researchers conducted an experiment in which participants were exposed to differently framed messages (gain-framed vs. loss-framed) and different price endings (round vs. odd). In the context of health club memberships, the research team used, for example, "Don't miss out on buying your six-pack from us with $40/mo." as loss-framed slogan with even pricing and "Buy your six-pack from us with $39/mo." as gain-framed slogan with odd-price ending. Results showed that gain-framed messages were more effective in the case of odd prices but did not change purchase likelihood when the price was round. Odd pricing with gain-framed promotions received the highest ratings across all price ending / frame combinations.

If prices are odd, frame promotions as gains ("gain $x") instead of reduced losses ("save $x").

Odd Pricing: Location of Copy Text

You are about to design an advertisement. The copy section is written and an odd price is chosen. Now you decide whether to place the price to the left or to the right of the verbal section. What would be your decision?

Coulter (2002) rationalized that the right part of the brain processes price information more efficiently than the left hemisphere. The researcher concluded consumers perceive prices as lower if subconsciously processed via the right brain part because it requires less mental effort. As visual nerves are connected to the opposite part of the brain, prices on the left-hand side of an ad should be processed by the right part of the brain. To increase the degree of subconscious processing of prices via the right hemisphere, the left-brain part should be actively engaged – e.g. by reading and understanding a verbal part on an advertisement. In addition, the researcher argued for a positive price image effect accompanying odd prices and that this effect is strongest if price is communicated on the left-hand side.

To test these hypotheses, the researcher ran an experiment: Coulter (2002) placed prices either on the left or the right of an ad next to a verbal section and used either odd or round prices.

When participants were asked about the likelihood that the advertised product was a bargain and their propensity to choose it, they gave highest ratings when an odd price was presented to the left of a verbal section.

Place odd prices on the left-hand side of a verbal section.

Price Increases and Communication

The only convenience store in your immediate neighborhood increased prices by about 10% across its whole assortment without any notice. What do you think? You might infer that the store takes advantage of its local monopolistic power. What would you think if the store announced that this is the first price increase in five years and the average inflation rate was between 2% and 3% in each of the last five years?

When companies increase prices, consumers infer motives and rationale behind this change. Price changes that consumers believe managers made to increase profit or to take advantage of a rise in demand are considered as unfair, whereas price increases that are caused by cost increases, which companies cannot influence, are regarded as acceptable (Xia, Monroe, and Cox 2004).

This is particularly relevant as inflation puts upward pressure on cost and prices in general. However, people tend to underestimate the impact of inflation and attribute price increases to price gouging as Bolton, Warlop, and Alba (2003) found out.

The researchers conducted an experiment in which they described the former selling price of a retailer's product, the inflation rate he experienced and the current price. Participants were asked whether the current price was appropriate, too high or too low. Although the new price was set at a fair level (i.e. equaling to former price plus impact of

inflation), still 30% of participants underestimated the impact of inflation and suggested the fair price should be 18% lower. Only 8% over-
estimated the impact of inflation, while the remaining 62% agreed with
the fair price.

If the company had communicated better on the impact of unavoid-
able cost increases, about one-third of their customer base would not
evaluate the current price as unfair.

> *Explain why you increase prices when the root cause is an unavoida-*
> *ble cost increase (in particular due to inflation) as people might infer*
> *negative intentions otherwise.*

Price Discounts and Communication

You want to buy a T-shirt and come across the sale of a T-shirt for
$14.99 that is regularly priced at $20. How do you evaluate the plausibility of the offer and the attractiveness of the deal? How would your
evaluation change if it carried the headline "We purchased in high volumes and now we're passing the savings on to you!".

Multiple studies have confirmed that plausibility of a discount influences perceived savings (Krishna et al. 2002).

One way to stress plausibility of a discount is to provide a reason
why a discount is offered. Bobinski Jr, Cox, and Cox (1996) asked participants to rate an offer on attitude toward the offer, perceived value
of the deal and perceived credibility of the retailer. The offer showed
a sale price, randomly included a regular selling price and carried one
of the following rationales for the price discount: no rationale (control
condition), high-volume rationale ("We purchased in high volumes
and now we're passing the savings on to you!"), or inventory rationale
("Pre-inventory sale – We don't want to count it, so you save!").

When the researchers added a high-volume rationale headline, the
offer resulted in significantly higher attitude, credibility, and perceived
value ratings compared to either an inventory rationale or no rationale
at all. However, researchers could only demonstrate this effect when
the sale price was framed as a price discount relative to a regular selling

price. Without an external anchor, ratings were similar across all three rationale conditions.

Volume-induced reasons for discounts improve attitude toward the offer, perceived value of the deal, and credibility of the retailer – in particular, when the sale price is framed as price discount.

Temporal Reframing

Imagine you are selling insurance contracts that cost $100 per annum and are to be paid upfront. How do you think would customers react if you framed the price as 27 cents per day – although the actual price does not change and the same amount is immediately due?

Gourville (1998) found that stating a price as a smaller amount per time unit increases customers' purchase intentions. In an experiment, he exposed participants with a request for donation and solicited their likelihood of donation. One group of participants was asked for $350 per year, whereas for another group the amount was framed as "$1 per day." When asked for their willingness to donate, participants showed a higher likelihood when the price was temporally reframed ($1 per day) instead of aggregated ($350 per year).

Framing a price as (smaller) amount per time unit reduces magnitude perception ("pennies-a-day strategy").

When Temporal Reframing Works Best

The "pennies-a-day strategy" is not a silver bullet and is most effective under specific conditions.

The initial experiment on temporal reframing also showed that the effectiveness of the pennies-a-day strategy diminished when amounts increased from $350 framed as $1 per day to $1,400/$4 per day or $2,500/$7 per day (Gourville 1998). This indicates that temporal reframing is not universally effective and lends support to the existence of boundary conditions under which temporal reframing works best.

In a subsequent study, Gourville (1999) tested the impact of temporal reframing on continuously consumed (eg. mobile phone service or gym membership) vs. immediately consumed (eg. airplane ticket or hotel accommodation) products and the effect of explicit comparisons. In the explicit comparison condition, the price was compared to a concrete petty-cash expense – for example in the case of the mobile phone scenario: "For the Cost of Your Morning Coffee, Never Be Unreachable."

In an experiment, subjects were randomly exposed to an ad showing one of the possible 16 versions: Four products (two products for each consumption rate condition) x two frames (per day vs. aggregated) x two explicit comparison (yes vs. no). Subjects were asked to indicate their value perception of the particular deal. The experiment showed that

- For continuously consumed products, temporal reframing increases perceived value compared to aggregate prices. Adding an explicit comparison next to the aggregate price has the same effect whereas adding an explicit comparison to an already temporally reframed price has no additional impact.

  Temporal reframing or explicit comparisons work for continuously consumed products.

- For immediately consumed products, consumers prefer aggregate prices to temporally reframed prices. Adding explicit comparisons to temporally reframed prices of immediately consumed products significantly increased perceived value, however if this explicit comparison is added next to the aggregated price, perceived value drops significantly.

  For immediately consumed products, aggregated prices without any comparisons communicate the highest perceived value.

Bambauer-Sachse and Grewal (2011) followed up on this research and looked at the impact of four factors determining the effectiveness of reframing prices: price endings (odd vs. even), price levels (low vs.

high), normal consumption periods (short vs. long) and the consumer's calculation affinity in the context of continuously consumed products.

The research team documented following findings:

- Price endings: In an experiment in the context of health club memberships, participants reported higher purchase intentions when temporally reframed prices were presented with even endings (€15 per week or €2 per day) compared to odd endings (€14.99 per week or €1.99 per day). The opposite holds true for aggregate amounts: respondents preferred odd price (€59.99) to even prices (€60) and indicated a higher purchase intent.

  Round prices work better for reframed prices and odd prices for aggregate amounts.

- Price levels: In this experiment, the research team presented products with different price levels: Internet flat rate contract (€24 per month) and a car leasing contract (€240 per month). Results showed that for lower prices, consumers prefer aggregate amounts to daily/weekly reframed prices stating higher purchase intentions. For high prices, consumers exhibited a higher likelihood to purchase when the price was temporally reframed instead of aggregate.

  Reframed prices work better for high prices and aggregate prices for low prices.

- Normal consumption period: Testing the impact of the normal consumption period on the effectiveness of temporal reframing on purchase intentions, the researchers presented two products identically priced per year: monthly health club membership (€60) and annual car insurance (€720). Results demonstrated consumer are more likely to purchase products with a long consumption period when they are presented aggregate prices instead of temporally reframed. For products with shorter

consumption periods, participants indicated a stronger preference for temporally reframed compared to aggregate prices.

*Reframed prices work better for short consumption periods and ag-
gregate prices for long consumption periods.*

The researchers also asked participants about their calculation affinity (e.g. "How strong do you agree / disagree with the following
statement: 'Mental arithmetic does not pose a problem for me.'"). The
researchers found that respondents with low calculation affinity exhibited higher purchase intentions when the price was reframed instead
of aggregated. On the other hand, consumers with high calculation affinity prefer aggregate to reframed prices.

*For products that are continuously consumed (e.g. mobile phone ser-
vice), temporal reframing works best. For immediately consumed
products (e.g. airplane ticket), aggregate prices are more effective.
When presenting temporal reframed prices, use even prices; for aggregate prices, use odd prices. For low price levels, aggregate prices;
for high price levels, temporally reframe prices. If the normal consumption period is short, reframe prices; for long consumption periods, aggregate prices.*

Price Multiples

You invite your friends to a pizza party at your favorite pizza chain.
Today, they run two promotions: "4 small pizzas, unlimited toppings
for $24" or "4 small pizzas, up to 6 toppings for $24." Which offer do
you order?

King and Janiszewski (2011) found that processing fluency drives
number liking. The researchers reasoned that consumers could easily
draw on results of common arithmetic operations (e.g. 2 + 2, 5 x 5) so
that there is a readily available association between single operands (2
+ 2) and the result (4) for these basic operations. Studying which numbers up to 100 consumers like more than other numbers, the research
team found that respondents like sum and product numbers in particular.

To test the hypothesis that people like prices more when they are primed as a basic arithmetic operations, King and Janiszewski (2011) presented participants in an experiment with promotional offers of a well-known pizza chain. The offers were "3 medium pizzas, up to 8 toppings," "4 small pizzas, up to 6 toppings," "3 medium pizzas, unlimited toppings," and "4 small pizzas, unlimited toppings," each one at a price of $24. Please note that the products of presented numbers (3 x 8, 4 x 6) in the first two offers equal to the price, 24. Respondents evaluated each offer. Results showed that consumers indeed rated the first two offers more favorably than the last two offers. This is particularly noteworthy as the last two offers ("unlimited toppings") are actually superior to the first ones.

Incorporate numbers into the ad that consumers easily arithmetically relate to the price.

Per-unit Pricing

You enter your favorite grocer to buy cereal. On the shelf, you find a dozen different brands with different package sizes and largely different prices. You do not have a favorite brand so you pick a pack that appears reasonably priced. When you are leaving the aisle, you look at the pack and find a price per ounce in addition to the price tag. Would you go back and compare offers again?

Miyazaki, Sprott, and Manning (2000) investigated the question how prominence of per-unit pricing affects customers' spending behavior. When retailers prominently displayed prices per unit, the researchers found that customers (a) prefer to buy products with a lower price per unit, (b) buy fewer products with a quantity surcharge for larger pack sizes (i.e. larger packs are more expensive per unit than smaller packs), and (c) do not buy more products. Overall, customers spend less for the same quantity of items. This finding is particularly interesting for retailers aiming to shift demand to their own private labels with attractive margins.

Shifting perspective from customers' purchase behavior in light of more or less prominent per-unit prices in a given retail outlet, Roth, Himbert, and Zielke (2017) analyzed how per-unit pricing affects the price image customers form of a retailer. The researchers found that consumers hold a more favorable price image of a retailer that states prices per unit, translating into higher shopping intentions with those retailers.

State prices per unit whenever possible.

Bottom Dollar Effect

Imagine you budgeted $100 this month for entertainment expenses. Now you have to decide about going to the cinema. Would it matter whether you are going to spend your first or your last $10 of your budget on a movie ticket?

Soster, Gershoff, and Bearden (2014) analyzed this question and found that consumers were averse to deplete their budget with a given transaction and were much more dissatisfied with their purchase if they did.

The researchers suggested when you plan your marketing campaigns you should take into account the level of your customers' budget.

For example, if the goal of your campaign is to acquire new, satisfied customers who try your product, you should start your campaign when budgets are still available – most likely at the beginning of a month.

On the other hand, when consumers' budgets approach depletion near the end of the month, they should become more sensitive to sale or coupon promotions.

Time your marketing campaigns with regard to your customers' budget levels. Consumers should accept product trial promotions at the beginning of a month, whereas sale promotions might be more effective at the end of a month.

Reciprocity Effect: Small Gifts

You enter a fast-food restaurant and the owner greets you with a warm welcome and a free desert. How do you feel toward the restaurant owner? Do you perceive a subtle need to give something back?

In his classic book on interpersonal relations and persuasion Cialdini (2014) defined the principle of reciprocity as follows: someone who received a gift or benefit from another person feels indebted so that he develops the need to give something back.

Applying the idea of reciprocity to pricing, Friedman and Rahman (2011) conducted the following field experiment. In a cooperating fast-food restaurant, the researchers randomly welcomed customers at entry with one of three different scenarios: (1) no welcome (control group), (2) greeting, or (3) greeting and a small gift (free yoghurt, also sold by the restaurant individually for 50 cents).

The researchers confirmed the reciprocity in a retail context. They found that customers spent on average $7.11 without any special welcome procedure, but spent $8.39 (+18% versus control group) when appreciatory greeting was used, and $10.41 (+46% versus control group) when warmly welcomed and handed a small gift.

Welcoming customers with warm words and small gifts instills feeling of indebtedness and increases willingness to spend.

Glucose Effect: Sweet Gifts

You are about to buy a piece of jewelry. The friendly representative offers you a free espresso and some chocolate. The chocolate melts in your mouth and you feel in the right mood to spend money – and you actually wonder why.

The "happiness hormone" serotonin increases people's likelihood to accept unfair offers in negotiation situations (Crockett et al. 2008).

Glucose, or simply "sugar", is an effective means to raise serotonin levels by triggering a chain of different substances released by the body – the glucose-insulin-tryptophan-serotonin chain (e.g. Benton 2002).

Linzmajer et al. (2014) supplied participants in an experiment randomly with sugar (pharmaceutical glucose dissolved in sparkling water).

Then the researchers presented 48 products with a price tag and asked subjects whether the price was fair, and, if it was not, participants could name a fair price.

Results showed that consumers who received the sugar drink regarded prices as fairer (share of unfair prices dropped from 28% to 15%) and were willing to pay about 17% higher prices.

One word on timing: the insulin level (and, therefore, also the serotonin level) shows two peaks after 10 and 40 minutes since sugar intake according to a standard insulin release curve for healthy adults (Suckale and Solimena 2008). The researchers measured price fairness perception after these 10 and 40 minutes and argued that outside these periods, the effect would not be significant.

Although serotonin levels are effective in letting customers perceive prices as fairer, the opposite is true for promotions. Mishra and Mishra (2010) demonstrated that a higher serotonin level reduced people's impulsivity and, thereby, their willingness to purchase a product that was on sale.

Treat consumers to sweets before presenting prices a few minutes later. Do not show discounted items that are on sale.

Money Back Guarantees

You are about to buy a mattress. Two models made it to your final round: After lying down on each of them for a few minutes, you do not see any difference. The first is $300. The second is $330 but comes with a money-back guarantee so you can return it without any hassles within 30 days if you are not satisfied.

Suwelack, Hogreve, and Hoyer (2011) studied the impact of money-back guarantees (MBGs) for search products and experience goods. For the former, consumers can evaluate product performance before purchase (e.g. washing machine), the latter are products that can only be evaluated after experiencing their consumption (e.g. haircut).

In experiments, the researchers observed the following impact of MBGs on participants' evaluations:

- MBGs reduced the performance risk and the financial risk that customers perceived before the purchase.

- MBGs reduced emotions of anticipated regret and lifted product liking.

- MBGs raised purchase intentions and willingness to pay.

- MBGs were more effective for experience than for search goods.

- MBGs that allowed consumers sufficient time to evaluate the good were more credible.

- Surprisingly, for experience goods, stricter MBGs increased perceived credibility compared to MBGs that were easier to invoke.

Overall, MBGs were found to increase consumers' likelihood to buy a product even at a higher price as long as the MBG is perceived as fair and credible.

Money back guarantees (MBGs) increase purchase likelihood and willingness to pay if consumers perceive them as fair and credible. A stricter MBG might even increase credibility perception.

CHAPTER 4

Price Payment Parameters

Price payment parameters describe the process of actually transferring money from buyers to sellers. This domain is relatively under researched so that only few studies focus on the impact of paying on customer perception and how it shapes customer behavior.

We will dive deeper on designing actual payments and look into three categories grouping eight effects:

1. *Payment Method* describes the impact of various types of money transfers on customer behavior – in particular the pain of payment people associate with different payment methods.
2. *Payment Currency* summarizes studies that look into how payment in different currencies affect customers' spending behavior.
3. *Payment Timing* refers to effects such as the temporal position of payments relative to consumption (pre-payments/post-payments) or the design of different payment schedules (e.g. increasing/decreasing installments).

Payment Method

Credit Card Effect

Have you ever noticed that you spend more easily when paying with a credit card? You are not alone.

During the process of paying, consumers experience pain (Prelec and Loewenstein 1998). However, this pain of payment is attenuated with the choice of payment method. Early studies already demonstrated a spending stimulating effect of credit cards (Feinberg 1986; Hirschman 1979). Paying by credit card increased consumers' willingness to pay by up to 100% relative to cash payments (Prelec and Simester 2001).

Soman (2003) clarified the underlying factors behind different degrees of pain caused by payment: Payment transparency – i.e. salience of actual payment and salience of paid amount – impacts spending behavior.

His research proposed the following ranking of payment transparency by payment method, with cash being most transparent: cash, check, credit card, debit card, stored-value card and autopay (direct debit from bank account).

In his field study, the researcher intercepted shoppers at a supermarket and asked them to leave their receipt for further analysis as part of an academic study. The researcher separated the receipts by payment method – cash: high transparency, check: medium transparency, credit card: low transparency – and coded items on the receipts as inflexible (staple grocery products with fixed consumption rate) or flexible (treats, luxuries) consumption products. The amount paid for inflexible products was statistically the same across all payment methods (between $23.88 and $24.77). But on flexible items, customers spend on average more when the payment method was low in transparency (credit card: $18.72) compared with medium transparency (check: $11.71) or high transparency (cash: $9.08).

In comparison to cash payments, individuals spend over 100% more with their credit cards for items that were not necessary.

With technological advances, more convenient and less transparent payment methods (e.g. Apple Pay) emerge that potentially drive spending behavior and willingness to pay.

Monopoly Money Effect

It is your birthday and your friends chip in to make you a present. They make you a money gift of $100 beautifully arranged in bills. You take the money and go shopping in your favorite mall. How easily do you part with the cash presented? How would your spending behavior change if the gift had not been cash but a gift card?

Raghubir and Srivastava (2008) conducted a field experiment with students participating in a bogus study. As part of this experiment, students received $1 as appreciation for their time invested in the fake study. The money would be handed over in cash or on a gift card. At the end of the study, students were asked to spend the money received on candy or – in case of the gift card – exchange it for a $1 bill.

When the $1 was handed over in cash 18% of participants decided to spend it on candy whereas 50% of subjects receiving $1 as gift card did.

In this field study and additional experiments, the researchers demonstrated that consumers part more easily with money when spent via less transparent payment methods – they would treat it like "monopoly money."

Give consumers the opportunity to convert cash into less transparent payment methods (e.g. incentivize prepaid credits with bulk discounts, promote gift cards).

Denomination Effect or Bias for the Whole

You go shopping. In your wallet, you find five $20 bills. In the first store, you notice that a T-shirt of your favorite brand is on sale for

$19.95. Do you spontaneously buy it? How would you decide if your wallet contained a $100 bill instead of five $20 bills?

In various studies, research demonstrated that consumers are less likely to part with money of larger denominations – an effect called bias for the whole (Mishra, Mishra, and Nayakankuppam 2006) or denomination effect (Raghubir and Srivastava 2009). Even when people have the same total amount of money at their disposal, consumers show a higher willingness to pay when the money available is split into smaller parts. This means, consumers would spend more if they carry 10 $10 bills compared with one $100 bill or four quarters instead of a $1 bill. Raghubir and Srivastava (2009) invited students to a "decoy experiment," thanked them for their participation and gave each participant $1. Students were told they could keep the dollar or spend it on candy (priced between 25 cents and $2). One-half of participants received a $1 bill, whereas the other half received four quarters. Sixty-three percent of subjects in the small denomination condition bought some candy, but only 26% of the large denomination group did so.

A reason for this effect is that larger denominations are easier to process so that spending money in larger denominations becomes more salient and, thereby, "painful" (Mishra, Mishra, and Nayakankuppam 2006). Therefore, people strategically choose to receive money in larger denominations to support their self-control on spending behavior (Raghubir and Srivastava 2009).

Present prices in smaller denominations ("just four quarters") or return change in smaller units of currency.

Payment Currency

Face Value Effect in Different Currencies

Research in behavioral economics repeatedly documented an effect called "money illusion" (Fisher 1928; Shafir, Diamond, and Tversky 1997). Researchers found that people base their economic decisions on nominal rather than real terms, systematically neglecting or underestimating the impact of inflation or deflation.

Extending these findings to prices in different currencies, Raghubir and Srivastava (2002) identified a face-value effect: People tend to anchor on the numerical value of the home currency and insufficiently adjust for the exchange rate. If the target currency is a multiple of the home currency (e.g. $1US = 8.5 Norwegian krone) then people anchor on the smaller home currency amount and express a lower willingness to pay leading to underspending. The effect reverses if the target currency is a fraction of the home currency (e.g. $1US = 0.4 Bahraini dinar). In this low numerosity scenario, consumers tend also to anchor on the higher home currency amount and show a tendency for overspending.

Introducing a fixed budget expressed in the target currency, Wertenbroch, Soman, and Chattopadhyay (2007) demonstrate that the face value effect reverses. People tend to consider the amount left after the spending decision instead of the face value of the price. In experimental studies, researchers showed that consumers prefer a price of $A 100 in light of a budget of $A 1,000 over a price of $B 1 in light of a budget of $B 10 because the amount left in the former case is $A 900 and, thus, more numerous than $B 9 in the latter case.

The face value of the currency matters. If you introduce a new currency (e.g. in a loyalty program) so that customers can earn this currency, build up a budget, and spend it on offered items, you should choose an exchange rate that is a multiple of your customers' home currency.

Combined Currencies Effect

Assume you are a member of an airline's frequent-flyer program. You decide to take a few days off and fly to Hawaii. The flight costs $1,000 and you can either pay with dollars; dollars and miles ($500 plus 25,000 miles); or just with miles (50,000 miles). Which payment option do you prefer? How would your decision about the payment method change if it was a short flight costing either $150; $75 plus $3,750 miles; or $7,500 miles?

Drèze and Nunes (2004) revealed theoretically and experimentally specific price ranges for which paying with money only, points only, or a combination of money and points would be preferred by customers as it minimizes pain of payment. In a field experiment, the researchers approached actual passengers in an airport waiting for departure. Volunteering participants stated the price of the ticket of their current journey. Then the researchers transferred the dollar amount into miles (exchange rate $0.02 per mile) and asked subjects whether they preferred paying with money only, miles only or a combination (50%/50%).

Research showed that for ticket prices below $300 participants preferred money-only payments, for ticket prices between $300 and $1,200 preferences changed to mixed payments, and subjects preferred miles-only payments for ticket prices above $1,200.

Drèze and Nunes (2004) demonstrated introducing an additional currency (e.g. points, miles) and allowing mixed-currency payments can maximize revenue compared to either single currency (i.e. only points or only money).

Introduce an additional currency (e.g. miles as part of your loyalty program) and allow mixed currency payments.

Payment Timing

Level of Installments

You finance a new car. Which financing plan would you prefer – a plan with constant, decreasing, or increasing installments?

Research confirmed that people like sequences of improving outcomes (Loewenstein and Prelec 1993). Based on this finding Peine, Wentzel, and Herrmann (2012) tested the hypothesis that customers might prefer decreasing levels of installments over constant or increasing amounts of installments. The research team invited potential car buyers on the website of a European car manufacturer to participate in an online survey. In this experiment, participants were exposed to different installment plans over the course of four years. The monthly installments would be either constant, increasing, or decreasing. In the latter two cases, payments were the same for a whole year and changed after 12 months. The net present values were the same for all scenarios.

The experiment showed that customers were more willing to accept the offer in the case of decreasing installments than when the payments were ascending or constant.

If payment involves multiple installments (e.g. financing), steadily decrease the installments in the future.

Prepayments or Postpayments

For your holidays, you plan to embark on a cruise in the Caribbean. The travel agency offers you two different payment schemes: You can pay six installments in advance or you pay in six installments after the vacation without additional interest. Which payment scheme would you choose? You recognize that the latter is economically the right decision, but you wonder whether you would enjoy the vacation less compared to paying in advance. How would your decision change if you were about to buy a washing machine?

Prelec and Loewenstein (1998) reasoned that consumers experience pain from payments and benefits from actual consumption. The researchers further concluded that consumers would keep track of pain and benefits separately and predicted that individuals strictly avoid getting into red – i.e. people avoid situations when pain exceeds benefits.

The researchers also suggested that consumers do not experience pain of paying and benefits from consuming independently. The reasons were two-fold. First, at the time of payment, thoughts about future benefits derived from the purchase buffer any pain of payment. Second, at the time of consumption consumers spend little to no thoughts about the payment so that they enjoy consumption as it were free.

Based on those assumptions, consumers should prefer prepayments for products with a short consumption period – like vacations. For those products, if payments are after consumption, there are no further benefits that could compensate pain of payments and bring total utility back to black. For durable products, consumers might prefer later payments as those still face periods of consumption and benefits. In those cases, people should prefer post-payments as these are economically more reasonable – i.e. have a lower net present value of payments.

Participants in an experiment were asked to choose between two payment schemes: paying six installments before (a vacation) [arrival of clothes washer and dryer] or paying six installments after (a vacation) [arrival of clothes washer and dryer].

Results showed that participants preferred prepayments for a vacation (60%) but post-payments for a washer-dryer combination (84%).

These findings also explain why consumers prefer a loan with a duration matching the life of the financed durable (Hirst, Joyce, and Schadewald 1994).

Consumers prefer prepayments for products with a short-consumption period and post-payments for durables during their consumption period.

Payment Timing and Consumption

Consumers have a hedonic inclination to pay in advance – but what is the impact of prepayments on actual consumption? Research showed that consumers obey sunk costs. Sunk costs are costs that incurred in the past and should no longer impact current decisions, for example, about consumption. Thaler (1980) illustrated consumers' avoidance of sunk cost by increasing consumption with the following, fictitious example: A family would rather drive through a snowstorm to a basketball game when they paid for the tickets, but would probably stay at home if they were given tickets for free.

However, this tendency for increased consumption disappears over time as price paid and sunk cost depreciate. Arkes and Blumer (1985) found that theater customers who paid for their tickets in advance would on average go to 40% fewer plays in the second half of the season compared with the first. The researchers also found that the number of attended plays in the first half depended on the price customers paid: the higher the price, the more plays customers would attend. For the second half of the season, price no longer influenced attendance. Similarly, Gourville and Soman (1998) empirically demonstrate this depreciation effect by showing that customers of a health club exhibited an 83% lower attendance five months after their initial prepayment for one year.

Consumers are less likely to consume the product as time passes between payment and actual consumption.

References

Adaval, Rashmi and Kent B. Monroe (2002), "Automatic Construction and Use of Contextual Information for Product and Price Evaluations," *Journal of Consumer Research*, 28 (4), 572–588.

Ailawadi, Kusum L., Karen Gedenk, Tobias Langer, Yu Ma, and Scott A. Neslin (2014), "Consumer Response to Uncertain Promotions. An Empirical Analysis of Conditional Rebates," *International Journal of Research in Marketing*, 31 (1), 94–106.

Anderson, Chris K. (2009), "Setting Prices on Priceline," *Interfaces*, 39 (4), 307–315.

Anderson, Eric T. and Duncan I. Simester (2001), "Are Sale Signs Less Effective When More Products Have Them?" *Marketing Science*, 20 (2), 121.

——— (2003), "Effects of $9 Price Endings on Retail Sales. Evidence from Field Experiments," *Quantitative Marketing & Economics*, 1 (1), 93–110.

Ariely, Dan (2010), *Predictably Irrational. The Hidden Forces That Shape Our Decisions*. New York, NY: Harper Perennial.

Ariely, Dan, George F. Loewenstein, and Dražen Prelec (2003), "Coherent Arbitrariness: Stable Demand Curves Without Stable Preferences," *Quarterly Journal of Economics*, 118 (1), 73.

Arkes, Hal R. and Catherine Blumer (1985), "The Psychology of Sunk Cost," *Organizational Behavior and Human Decision Processes*, 35 (1), 124–140.

Babad, Elisha and Yosi Katz (1991), "Wishful Thinking — Against All Odds," *Journal of Applied Social Psychology*, 21 (23), 1921–1938.

Babin, Barry J., David M. Hardesty, and Tracy A. Suter (2003), "Color and Shopping Intentions. The Intervening Effect of Price Fairness and Perceived Affect," *Journal of Business Research*, 56 (7), 541–551.

Bagchi, Rajesh and Amar Cheema (2013), "The Effect of Red Background Color on Willingness-to-Pay. The Moderating Role of Selling Mechanism," *Journal of Consumer Research*, 39 (5), 947–960.

Bagchi, Rajesh and Derick F. Davis (2012), "$29 for 70 Items or 70 Items for $29? How Presentation Order Affects Package Perceptions," *Journal of Consumer Research*, 39 (1), 62–73.

Baker, Walter L., Michael V. Marn, and Craig C. Zawada (2010), *The Price Advantage. Wiley finance*. Hoboken, NJ: Wiley.

Balachander, Subramanian, Yan Liu, and Axel Stock (2009), "An Empirical Analysis of Scarcity Strategies in the Automobile Industry," *Management Science*, 55 (10), 1623–1637.

Bambauer-Sachse, Silke and Dhruv Grewal (2011), "Temporal Reframing of Prices: When Is It Beneficial?" *Journal of Retailing*, 87 (2), 156–165.

Barone, Michael, Keith Lyle, and Karen P. Winterich (2015), "When Deal Depth Doesn't Matter. How Handedness Consistency Influences Consumer Response to Horizontal Versus Vertical Price Comparisons," *Marketing Letters*, 26 (2), 213–223.

Bellizzi, Joseph A. and Robert E. Hite (1992), "Environmental Color, Consumer Feelings, and Purchase Likelihood," *Psychology & Marketing*, 9 (5), 347–363.

Benton, David (2002), "Carbohydrate Ingestion, Blood Glucose and Mood," *Neuroscience & Biobehavioral Reviews*, 26 (3), 293–308.

Bertini, Marco and Luc Wathieu (2008), "Attention Arousal Through Price Partitioning," *Marketing Science*, 27 (2), 236–246.

Bertini, Marco, Luc Wathieu, and Sheena S. Iyengar (2012), "The Discriminating Consumer. Product Proliferation and Willingness to Pay for Quality," *Journal of Marketing Research*, 49 (1), 39–49.

Biswas, Abhijit, Sandeep Bhowmick, Abhijit Guha, and Dhruv Grewal (2013), "Consumer Evaluations of Sale Prices: Role of the Subtraction Principle," *Journal of Marketing*, 77 (4), 49–66.

Biswas, Abhijit and Scot Burton (1993), "Consumer Perceptions of Tensile Price Claims in Advertisements. An Assessment of Claim Types Across Different Discount Levels," *Journal of the Academy of Marketing Science*, 21 (3), 217–229.

——— (1994), "An Experimental Assessment of Effects Associated with Alternative Tensile Price Claims," *Journal of Business Research*, 29 (1), 65–73.

Blair, Edward A. and E. L. Landon Jr. (1981), "The Effects of Reference Prices in Retail Advertisements," *Journal of Marketing*, 45 (2), 61–69.

Bobinski Jr, George S., Dena Cox, and Anthony Cox (1996), "Retail "Sale" Advertising, Perceived Retailer Credibility and Price Rationale," *Consumer Behavior and Retailing*, 72 (3), 291–306.

Bolton, Lisa E., Luk Warlop, and Joseph W. Alba (2003), "Consumer Perceptions of Price (Un)Fairness," *Journal of Consumer Research*, 29 (4), 474–491.

Brough, Aaron R. and Alexander Chernev (2012), "When Opposites Detract: Categorical Reasoning and Subtractive Valuations of Product Combinations," *Journal of Consumer Research*, 39 (2), 399–414.

Brysbaert, Marc (1995), "Arabic Number Reading. On the Nature of the Numerical Scale and the Origin of Phonological Recoding," *Journal of Experimental Psychology*, 124 (4), 434–452.

Burman, Bidisha and Abhijit Biswas (2007), "Partitioned Pricing: Can We Always Divide and Prosper?" *Journal of Retailing*, 83 (4), 423–436.

Cai, Fengyan, Hao Shen, and Michael K. Hui (2012), "The Effect of Location on Price Estimation. Understanding Number-Location and Number-Order Associations," *Journal of Marketing Research*, 49 (5), 718–724.

Cai, Fengyan, Felix Tang, and Jian-Min Jia (2009), "The Interaction Effect of Mood and Price Level on Purchase Intention," *Advances in Consumer Research*, 36, 963–965.

Çakır, Metin and Joseph V. Balagtas (2014), "Consumer Response to Package Downsizing. Evidence from the Chicago Ice Cream Market," *Consumer Behavior and Retailing*, 90 (1), 1–12.

Carpenter, Gregory S., Rashi Glazer, and Kent Nakamoto (1994), "Meaningful Brands from Meaningless Differentiation. The Dependence on Irrelevant Attributes," *Journal of Marketing Research*, 31 (3), 339–350.

Chaiken, Shelly (1980), "Heuristic Versus Systematic Information Processing and the Use of Source Versus Message Cues in Persuasion," *Journal of Personality and Social Psychology*, 39 (5), 752–766.

Chakravarti, Dipankar, Rajan Krish, Pallab Paul, and Joydeep Srivastava (2002), "Partitioned Presentation of Multicomponent Bundle Prices. Evaluation, Choice and Underlying Processing Effects," *Journal of Consumer Psychology*, 12 (3), 215–229.

Chandon, Pierre and Nailya Ordabayeva (2009), "Supersize in One Dimension, Downsize in Three Dimensions: Effects of Spatial Dimensionality on Size Perceptions and Preferences," *Journal of Marketing Research*, 46 (6), 739–753.

Chandrashekaran, Rajesh and Dhruv Grewal (2006), "Anchoring Effects of Advertised Reference Price and Sale Price. The Moderating Role of Saving Presentation Format," *Journal of Business Research*, 59 (10/11), 1063–1071.

Chang, Tung-Zong and Albert R. Wildt (1996), "Impact of Product Information on the Use of Price as a Quality Cue," *Psychology & Marketing*, 13 (1), 55–75.

Cheema, Amar and Dilip Soman (2006), "Malleable Mental Accounting. The Effect of Flexibility on the Justification of Attractive Spending and Consumption Decisions," *Journal of Consumer Psychology*, 16 (1), 33–44.

Chen, Haipeng, Howard Marmorstein, Michael Tsiros, and Akshay R. Rao (2012), "When More Is Less. The Impact of Base Value Neglect on Consumer Preferences for Bonus Packs over Price Discounts," *Journal of Marketing*, 76 (4), 64–77.

Chen, Haipeng and Akshay R. Rao (2007), "When Two Plus Two Is Not Equal to Four. Errors in Processing Multiple Percentage Changes," *Journal of Consumer Research*, 34 (3), 327–340.

Chen, Shih-Fen S., Kent B. Monroe, and Yung-Chien Lou (1998), "The Effects of Framing Price Promotion Messages on Consumers' Perceptions and Purchase Intentions," *Research Perspective on Retail Pricing*, 74 (3), 353–372.

Chen, Yuxin, Oded Koenigsberg, and Z. J. Zhang (2017), "Pay-as-You-Wish Pricing," *Marketing Science*, 36 (5), 780–791.

Cheng, Lillian L. and Kent B. Monroe (2013), "An Appraisal of Behavioral Price Research (Part 1): Price as a Physical Stimulus," *AMS Review*, 3 (3), 103–129.

Choi, Jungsil, Kiljae Lee, and Yong-Yeon Ji (2012), "What Type of Framing Message Is More Appropriate with Nine-Ending Pricing?" *Marketing Letters*, 23 (3), 603–614.

Choi, Pilsik and Keith S. Coulter (2012), "It's Not All Relative: The Effects of Mental and Physical Positioning of Comparative Prices on Absolute Versus Relative Discount Assessment," *Journal of Retailing*, 88 (4), 512–527.

Cialdini, Robert B. (2014), *Influence. Science and Practice. Always learning.* Harlow, Essex: Pearson.

Coulter, Keith S. (2002), "The Influence of Print Advertisement Organization on Odd-ending Price Image Effects," *Journal of Product and Brand Management*, 11 (5), 319–334.

Coulter, Keith S., Pilsik Choi, and Kent B. Monroe (2012), "Comma N' Cents in Pricing: The Effects of Auditory Representation Encoding on Price Magnitude Perceptions," *Journal of Consumer Psychology*, 22 (3), 395–407.

Coulter, Keith S. and Robin A. Coulter (2005), "Size Does Matter: The Effects of Magnitude Representation Congruency on Price Perceptions and Purchase Likelihood," *Journal of Consumer Psychology*, 15 (1), 64–76.

——— (2007), "Distortion of Price Discount Perceptions: The Right Digit Effect," *Journal of Consumer Research*, 34 (2), 162–173.

——— (2010), "Small Sounds, Big Deals. Phonetic Symbolism Effects in Pricing," *Journal of Consumer Research*, 37 (2), 315–328.

Coulter, Keith S. and Dhruv Grewal (2014), "Name-Letters and Birth-day-Numbers: Implicit Egotism Effects in Pricing," *Journal of Marketing*, 78 (3), 102–120.

Coulter, Keith S. and Patricia A. Norberg (2009), "The Effects of Physical Distance Between Regular and Sale Prices on Numerical Difference Perceptions," *Journal of Consumer Psychology*, 19 (2), 144–157.

Coulter, Keith S. and Anne L. Roggeveen (2014), "Price Number Relationships and Deal Processing Fluency. The Effects of Approximation Sequences and Number Multiples," *Journal of Marketing Research*, 51 (1), 69–82.

Crockett, Molly J., Luke Clark, Golnaz Tabibnia, Matthew D. Lieberman, and Trevor W. Robbins (2008), "Serotonin Modulates Behavioral Reactions to Unfairness," *Science*, 320 (5884), 1739.

Cunha Jr., Marcus and Jeffrey D. Shulman (2011), "Assimilation and Contrast in Price Evaluations," *Journal of Consumer Research*, 37 (5), 822–835.

Dehaene, Stanislas (1989), "The Psychophysics of Numerical Comparison: A Reexamination of Apparently Incompatible Data," *Perception & Psychophysics*, 45 (6), 557–566.

——— (1992), "Varieties of Numerical Abilities," *Numerical Cognition*, 44 (1–2), 1–42.

Dehaene, Stanislas, Emmanuel Dupoux, and Jacques Mehler (1990), "Is Numerical Comparison Digital? Analogical and Symbolic Effects in Two-Digit Number Comparison," *Journal of Experimental Psychology*, 16 (3), 626–641.

Dehaene, Stanislas and Jacques Mehler (1992), "Cross-Linguistic Regularities in the Frequency of Number Words," *Numerical Cognition*, 43 (1), 1–29.

DelVecchio, Devon, H. S. Krishnan, and Daniel C. Smith (2007), "Cents or Percent? The Effects of Promotion Framing on Price Expectations and Choice," *Journal of Marketing*, 71 (3), 158–170.

DelVecchio, Devon, Arun Lakshmanan, and H. S. Krishnan (2009), "The Effects of Discount Location and Frame on Consumers' Price Estimates," *Consumer Behavior and Retailing*, 85 (3), 336–346.

Dhar, Ravi and Klaus Wertenbroch (2000), "Consumer Choice Between Hedonic and Utilitarian Goods," *Journal of Marketing Research*, 37 (1), 60–71.

Dobson, John, Larry Gorman, and Melissa D. Moore (2010), "Consumer Choice Bias Due to Number Symmetry. Evidence from Real Estate Prices," *Journal of Research for Consumers* (17), 1–12.

Doyle, John R., David J. O'Connor, Gareth M. Reynolds, and Paul A. Bottomley (1999), "The Robustness of the Asymmetrically Dominated Effect. Buying Frames, Phantom Alternatives, and in-Store Purchases," *Psychology & Marketing*, 16 (3), 225–243.

Drèze, Xavier and Joseph C. Nunes (2004), "Using Combined-Currency Prices to Lower Consumers' Perceived Cost," *Journal of Marketing Research*, 41 (1), 59–72.

Drumwright, Minette E. (1992), "A Demonstration of Anomalies in Evaluations of Bundling," *Marketing Letters*, 3 (4), 311–321.

Engeset, Marit G. and Birger Opstad (2017), "Evaluation Effects of Bundle Size and Price Presentation," *Journal of Consumer Marketing*, 34 (5), 393–403.

Estelami, Hooman (2003), "The Effect of Price Presentation Tactics on Consumer Evaluation Effort of Multi-Dimensional Prices," *Journal of Marketing Theory & Practice*, 11 (2), 1.

Feinberg, Richard A. (1986), "Credit Cards as Spending Facilitating Stimuli. A Conditioning Interpretation," *Journal of Consumer Research*, 13 (3), 348–356.

Feng, Shan, Rajneesh Suri, Mike C.-H. Chao, and Umit Koc (2017), "Presenting Comparative Price Promotions Vertically or Horizontally. Does It Matter?" *Journal of Business Research*, 76 (Supplement C), 209–218.

Fisher, Irving (1928), *The Money Illusion*. New York: Adelphi.

Friedman, Hershey H. and Ahmed Rahman (2011), "Gifts-Upon-Entry and Appreciatory Comments. Reciprocity Effects in Retailing," *International Journal of Marketing Studies*, 3 (3).

Gabler, Colin B. and Kristy E. Reynolds (2013), "Buy Now or Buy Later: The Effects of Scarcity and Discounts on Purchase Decisions," *Journal of Marketing Theory & Practice*, 21 (4), 441–456.

Gendall, Philip, Michael F. Fox, and Priscilla Wilton (1998), "Estimating the Effect of Odd Pricing," *Journal of Product and Brand Management*, 7 (5), 421.

Gierl, Heribert and Verena Huettl (2010), "Are Scarce Products Always More Attractive? The Interaction of Different Types of Scarcity Signals with Products' Suitability for Conspicuous Consumption," *International Journal of Research in Marketing*, 27 (3), 225–235.

Ginzberg, Eli (1936), "Customary Prices," *The American Economic Review*, 26 (2), 296.

Gourville, John T. (1998), "Pennies-a-Day: The Effect of Temporal Reframing on Transaction Evaluation," *Journal of Consumer Research*, 24 (4), 395–408.

———— (1999), "The Effect of Implicit Versus Explicit Comparisons on Temporal Pricing Claims," *Marketing Letters*, 10 (2), 113–124.

Gourville, John T. and Dilip Soman (1998), "Payment Depreciation. The Behavioral Effects of Temporally Separating Payments from Consumption," *Journal of Consumer Research*, 25 (2), 160–174.

Greenleaf, Eric A. (1995), "The Impact of Reference Price Effect on the Profitability of Price Promotions," *Marketing Science*, 14 (1), 82.

Grewal, Dhruv and Howard Marmorstein (1994), "Market Price Variation, Perceived Price Variation, and Consumers' Price Search Decisions for Durable Goods," *Journal of Consumer Research*, 21 (3), 453–460.

Grewal, Dhruv, Howard Marmorstein, and Arun Sharma (1996), "Communicating Price Information Through Semantic Cues. The Moderating Effects of Situation and Discount Size," *Journal of Consumer Research*, 23 (2), 148–155.

Grewal, Dhruv, Anne L. Roggeveen, and Joan Lindsey-Mullikin (2014), "The Contingent Effects of Semantic Price Cues," *Consumer Behavior and Retailing*, 90 (2), 198–205.

Hamilton, Rebecca W. and Joydeep Srivastava (2008), "When 2 + 2 Is Not the Same as 1 + 3. Variations in Price Sensitivity Across Components of Partitioned Prices," *Journal of Marketing Research*, 45 (4), 450–461.

Harris, Judy and Edward A. Blair (2012), "Consumer Processing of Bundled Prices. When Do Discounts Matter?" *Journal of Product and Brand Management*, 21 (3), 205–214.

Heath, Chip and Jack B. Soll (1996), "Mental Budgeting and Consumer Decisions," *Journal of Consumer Research*, 23 (1), 40–52.

Heath, Timothy B. and Subimal Chatterjee (1995), "Asymmetric Decoy Effects on Lower-Quality Versus Higher-Quality Brands: Meta-Analytic and Experimental Evidence," *Journal of Consumer Research*, 22 (3), 268–284.

Heath, Timothy B., Subimal Chatterjee, and Karen R. France (1995), "Mental Accounting and Changes in Price. The Frame Dependence of Reference Dependence," *Journal of Consumer Research*, 22 (1), 90–97.

Helson, Harry (1964), *Adaption-Level Theory. An Experimental and Systematic Approach to Behavior*. New York, NY: Harper and Row.

Henik, Avishai and Joseph Tzelgov (1982), "Is Three Greater Than Five. The Relation Between Physical and Semantic Size in Comparison Tasks," *Memory & Cognition*, 10 (4), 389–395.

Herr, Paul M. (1989), "Priming Price. Prior Knowledge and Context Effects," *Journal of Consumer Research*, 16 (1), 67–75.

Hirschman, Elizabeth C. (1979), "Differences in Consumer Purchase Behavior by Credit Card Payment System," *Journal of Consumer Research*, 6 (1), 58–66.

Hirst, D.Eric, Edward J. Joyce, and Michael S. Schadewald (1994), "Mental Accounting and Outcome Contiguity in Consumer-Borrowing Decisions," *Organizational Behavior and Human Decision Processes*, 58 (1), 136–152.

Hossain, Tanjim and John Morgan (2006), "...plus Shipping and Handling: Revenue (Non) Equivalence in Field Experiments on EBay," *B.E. Journal of Economic Analysis & Policy: Advances in Economic Analysis & Policy*, 6 (2), 1–27.

Hu, Ye and Xin Wang (2010), "Country-of-Origin Premiums for Retailers in International Trades. Evidence from EBay's International Markets," *Consumer Behavior and Retailing*, 86 (2), 200–207.

Huber, Joel, John W. Payne, and Christopher P. Puto (1982), "Adding Asymmetrically Dominated Alternatives. Violations of Regularity and the Similarity Hypothesis," *Journal of Consumer Research*, 9 (1), 90–98.

——— (2014), "Let's Be Honest About the Attraction Effect," *Journal of Marketing Research*, 51 (4), 520–525.

Huber, Joel and Christopher P. Puto (1983), "Market Boundaries and Product Choice. Illustrating Attraction and Substitution Effects," *Journal of Consumer Research*, 10 (1), 31–44.

Husemann-Kopetzky, Markus and Sören Köcher (2017), "Price Endings That Matter. A Conceptual Replication of Implicit Egotism Effects in Pricing," *Journal of Marketing Behavior*, 2 (4), 313–324.

Inman, J. J. and Leigh McAlister (1993), "A Retailer Promotion Policy Model Considering Promotion Signal Sensitivity," *Marketing Science*, 12 (4), 339.

Inman, J. J., Leigh McAlister, and Wayne D. Hoyer (1990), "Promotion Signal. Proxy for a Price Cut?" *Journal of Consumer Research*, 17 (1), 74–81.

Inman, J. J., Anil C. Peter, and Priya Raghubir (1997), "Framing the Deal. The Role of Restrictions in Accentuating Deal Value," *Journal of Consumer Research*, 24 (1), 68–79.

Iyengar, Sheena S. and Mark R. Lepper (2000), "When Choice Is Demotivating. Can One Desire Too Much of a Good Thing?" *Journal of Personality and Social Psychology*, 79 (6), 995–1006.

Janiszewski, Chris and Marcus Cunha Jr. (2004), "The Influence of Price Discount Framing on the Evaluation of a Product Bundle," *Journal of Consumer Research*, 30 (4), 534–546.

Janiszewski, Chris and Donald R. Lichtenstein (1999), "A Range Theory Account of Price Perception," *Journal of Consumer Research*, 25 (4), 353–368.

Janiszewski, Chris and Dan Uy (2008), "Precision of the Anchor Influences the Amount of Adjustment," *Psychological Science*, 19 (2), 121–127.

Johnson, Michael D., Andreas Herrmann, and Hans H. Bauer (1999), "The Effects of Price Bundling on Consumer Evaluations of Product Offerings," *International Journal of Research in Marketing*, 16 (2), 129–142.

Jones, John T., Matthew C. Mirenberg, Brett W. Pelham, and Mauricio Carvallo (2004), "How Do I Love Thee? Let Me Count the Js: Implicit Egotism and Interpersonal Attraction," *Journal of Personality and Social Psychology*, 87 (5), 665–683.

Kahneman, Daniel and Amos Tversky (1979), "Prospect Theory. An Analysis of Decision Under Risk," *Econometrica*, 47 (2), 263–291.

Kalyanaram, Gurumurthy and Russell S. Winer (1995), "Empirical Generalizations from Reference Price Research," *Marketing Science*, 14 (3), G161.

Karmarkar, Uma R., Baba Shiv, and Brian Knutson (2015), "Cost Conscious? The Neural and Behavioral Impact of Price Primacy on Decision Making," *Journal of Marketing Research*, 52 (4), 467–481.

Khan, Uzma and Ravi Dhar (2010), "Price-Framing Effects on the Purchase of Hedonic and Utilitarian Bundles," *Journal of Marketing Research*, 47 (6), 1090–1099.

Kim, Hyeong and Thomas Kramer (2006), ""Pay 80%" Versus "Get 20% Off" The Effect of Novel Discount Presentation on Consumers' Deal Perceptions," *Marketing Letters*, 17 (4), 311–321.

Kim, Hyeong M. (2006), "The Effect of Salience on Mental Accounting. How Integration Versus Segregation of Payment Influences Purchase Decisions," *Journal of Behavioral Decision Making*, 19 (4), 381–391.

Kim, Jongmin, Nathan Novemsky, and Ravi Dhar (2013), "Adding Small Differences Can Increase Similarity and Choice," *Psychological Science*, 24 (2), 225–229.

Kim, Jungkeun (2017), "The Influence of Graphical Versus Numerical Information Representation Modes on the Compromise Effect," *Marketing Letters*, 28 (3), 397–409.

Kim, Jungkeun, Raghunath S. Rao, Kyeongheui Kim, and Akshay R. Rao (2011), "More or Less. A Model and Empirical Evidence on Preferences for Under- and Overpayment in Trade-in Transactions," *Journal of Marketing Research*, 48 (1), 157–171.

Kim, Ju-Young, Martin Natter, and Martin Spann (2009), "Pay What You Want. A New Participative Pricing Mechanism," *Journal of Marketing*, 73 (1), 44–58.

——— (2014), "Sampling, Discounts or Pay-What-You-Want. Two Field Experiments," *International Journal of Research in Marketing*, 31 (3), 327–334.

King, Dan and Chris Janiszewski (2011), "The Sources and Consequences of the Fluent Processing of Numbers," *Journal of Marketing Research*, 48 (2), 327–341.

Klein, George S. (1964), "Semantic Power Measured Through the Interference of Words with Color-Naming," *The American Journal of Psychology*, 77 (4), 576–588.

Kohli, Chiranjeev and Rajneesh Suri (2011), "The Price Is Right? Guidelines for Pricing to Enhance Profitability," *Business Horizons*, 54 (6), 563–573.

Koschate-Fischer, Nicole, Adamantios Diamantopoulos, and Katharina Oldenkotte (2012), "Are Consumers Really Willing to Pay More for a Favorable Country Image? A Study of Country-of-Origin Effects on Willingness to Pay," *Journal of International Marketing*, 20 (1), 19–41.

Koschate-Fischer, Nicole and Katharina Wüllner (2017), "New Developments in Behavioral Pricing Research," *Journal of Business Economics*, 87 (6), 809–875.

Krämer, Florentin, Klaus M. Schmidt, Martin Spann, and Lucas Stich (2017), "Delegating Pricing Power to Customers. Pay What You Want or Name Your Own Price?" *Journal of Economic Behavior & Organization*, 136, 125–140.

Krider, Robert E., Priya Raghubir, and Aradhna Krishna (2001), "Pizzas. Π or Square? Psychophysical Biases in Area Comparisons," *Marketing Science*, 20 (4), 405.

Krishna, Aradhna, Richard A. Briesch, Donald R. Lehmann, and Hong Yuan (2002), "A Meta-Analysis of the Impact of Price Presentation on Perceived Savings," *Journal of Retailing*, 78 (2), 101–118.

Krishnamurthy, Parthasarathy and Anish Nagpal (2010), "Making Choices Under Conflict. The Impact of Decision Frames," *Marketing Letters*, 21 (1), 37–51.

Krishnan, Balaji C., Abhijit Biswas, and Richard G. Netemeyer (2006), "Semantic Cues in Reference Price Advertisements. The Moderating Role of Cue Concreteness," *Journal of Retailing*, 82 (2), 95–104.

Krishnan, Balaji C., Sujay Dutta, and Subhash Jha (2013), "Effectiveness of Exaggerated Advertised Reference Prices: The Role of Decision Time Pressure," *Journal of Retailing*, 89 (1), 105–113.

Lambrecht, Anja and Bernd Skiera (2006), "Paying Too Much and Being Happy About It. Existence, Causes, and Consequences of Tariff-Choice Biases," *Journal of Marketing Research*, 43 (2), 212–223.

Leavitt, Harold J. (1954), "A Note on Some Experimental Findings About the Meanings of Price," *The Journal of Business*, 27 (3), 205–210.

Levin, Irwin P., Judy Schreiber, Marco Lauriola, and Gary J. Gaeth (2002), "A Tale of Two Ppzzas. Building up from a Basic Product Versus Scaling down from a Fully-Loaded Product," *Marketing Letters*, 13 (4), 335–344.

Lin, Chien-Huang and Jyh-Wen Wang (2017), "Distortion of Price Discount Perceptions Through the Left-Digit Effect," *Marketing Letters*, 28 (1), 99–112.

Linzmajer, Marc, Mirja Hubert, Tim Eberhardt, Thomas Fojcik, and Peter Kenning (2014), "The Effect of Glucose Consumption on Customers' Price Fairness Perception," *Schmalenbach Business Review*, 2014 (5), 7–49.

Liozu, Stephan M. and Andreas Hinterhuber (2013), "Pricing Orientation, Pricing Capabilities, and Firm Performance," *Management Decision*, 51 (3), 594–614.

Loewenstein, George F. and Dražen Prelec (1993), "Preferences for Sequences of Outcomes," *Psychological Review*, 100 (1), 91–108.

Love, Edwin (2012), "Divide and Prosper? When Partitioned Prices Make Sense," *Journal of Product and Brand Management*, 21 (1), 61–67.

Lowengart, Oded (2002), "Reference Price Conceptualisations. An Integrative Framework of Analysis," *Journal of Marketing Management*, 18 (1-2), 145–171.

Lowry, James R., Thomas A. Charles, and Judy A. Lane (2005), "A Comparison of Perceived Value Between a Percentage Markdown and a Monetary Markdown," *Marketing Management*, 15 (1), 140–148.

Lynn, Michael, Sean M. Flynn, and Chelsea Helion (2013), "Do Consumers Prefer Round Prices? Evidence from Pay-What-You-Want Decisions and Self-Pumped Gasoline Purchases," *Journal of Economic Psychology*, 36, 96–102.

Mandel, Naomi and Eric J. Johnson (2002), "When Web Pages Influence Choice. Effects of Visual Primes on Experts and Novices," *Journal of Consumer Research*, 29 (2), 235–245.

Marn, Michael V. and Robert L. Rosiello (1992), "Managing Price, Gaining Profit," *McKinsey Quarterly* (4), 18–37.

Marshall, Alfred (1890), *Principles of Economics*. London: Macmillan.

Mazumdar, Tridib and Sung Y. Jun (1993), "Consumer Evaluations of Multiple Versus Single Price Change," *Journal of Consumer Research*, 20 (3), 441–450.

Mazumdar, Tridib, S. P. Raj, and Indrajit Sinha (2005), "Reference Price Research: Review and Propositions," *Journal of Marketing*, 69 (4), 84–102.

McConnell, J. D. (1968), "The Price-Quality Relationship in an Experimental Setting," *Journal of Marketing Research*, 5 (3), 300–303.

Meyers-Levy, Joan and Durairaj Maheswaran (1991), "Exploring Differences in Males' and Females' Processing Strategies," *Journal of Consumer Research*, 18 (1), 63–70.

Mishra, Arul and Himanshu Mishra (2010), "We Are What We Consume. The Influence of Food Consumption on Impulsive Choice," *Journal of Marketing Research*, 47 (6), 1129–1137.

Mishra, Himanshu, Arul Mishra, and Dhananjay Nayakankuppam (2006), "Money. A Bias for the Whole," *Journal of Consumer Research*, 32 (4), 541–549.

Miyazaki, Anthony D., David E. Sprott, and Kenneth C. Manning (2000), "Unit Prices on Retail Shelf Labels. An Assessment of Information Prominence," *Consumer Behavior and Retailing*, 76 (1), 93.

Mogilner, Cassie and Jennifer Aaker (2009), ""The Time Vs. Money Effect" Shifting Product Attitudes and Decisions Through Personal Connection," *Journal of Consumer Research*, 36 (2), 277–291.

Monroe, Kent B. (1971a), "Measuring Price Thresholds by Psychophysics and Latitudes of Acceptance," *Journal of Marketing Research*, 8 (4), 460–464.

——— (1971b), "'psychophysics of Prices'. A Reappraisal," *Journal of Marketing Research*, 8 (2), 248–250.

——— (1973), "Buyers' Subjective Perceptions of Price," *Journal of Marketing Research*, 10 (1), 70–80.

Monroe, Kent B. and Angela V. Lee (1999), "Remembering Versus Knowing: Issues in Buyers' Processing of Price Information," *Journal of the Academy of Marketing Science*, 27 (2), 207–225.

Morwitz, Vicki G., Eric A. Greenleaf, and Eric J. Johnson (1998), "Divide and Prosper: Consumers' Reactions to Partitioned Prices," *Journal of Marketing Research*, 35 (4), 453–463.

Moyer, Robert S. and Thomas K. Landauer (1967), "Time Required for Judgements of Numerical Inequality," 215 (5109), 1519–1520.

Nagle, Thomas T., John Hogan, and Joseph Zale (2014), *The Strategy and Tactics of Pricing. A Guide to Growing More Profitably. Always learning.* Harlow: Pearson Education.

Ng, Travis, Terence Chong, and Xin Du (2010), "The Value of Superstitions," *Journal of Economic Psychology*, 31 (3), 293–309.

Nunes, Joseph C. and Peter Boatwright (2004), "Incidental Prices and Their Effect on Willingness to Pay," *Journal of Marketing Research*, 41 (4), 457–466.

Nunes, Joseph C. and C. W. Park (2003), "Incommensurate Resources: Not Just More of the Same," *Journal of Marketing Research*, 40 (1), 26–38.

Okada, Erica M. (2001), "Trade-Ins, Mental Accounting, and Product Replacement Decisions," *Journal of Consumer Research*, 27 (4), 433–446.

——— (2005), "Justification Effects on Consumer Choice of Hedonic and Utilitarian Goods," *Journal of Marketing Research*, 42 (1), 43–53.

Pauwels, Koen, Shuba Srinivasan, and Philip H. Franses (2007), "When Do Price Thresholds Matter in Retail Categories?" *Marketing Science*, 26 (1), 83–100.

Peine, Klaus, Daniel Wentzel, and Andreas Herrmann (2012), "Getting Better or Getting Worse? Consumer Responses to Decreasing, Constant, and Ascending Multi-Dimensional Price Profiles," *Review of Managerial Science*, 6 (1), 81–101.

Pelham, Brett W., Mauricio Carvallo, and John T. Jones (2005), "Implicit Egotism," *Current Directions in Psychological Science*, 14 (2), 106–110.

Pelham, Brett W., Matthew C. Mirenberg, and John T. Jones (2002), "Why Susie Sells Seashells by the Seashore: Implicit Egotism and Major Life Decisions," *Journal of Personality and Social Psychology*, 82 (4), 469–487.

Plassmann, Hilke, John O'Doherty, Baba Shiv, and Antonio Rangel (2008), "Marketing Actions Can Modulate Neural Representations of Experienced Pleasantness," *Proceedings of the National Academy of Sciences*, 105 (3), 1050–1054.

Prelec, Dražen and George F. Loewenstein (1998), "The Red and the Black: Mental Accounting of Savings and Debt," *Marketing Science*, 17 (1), 4.

Prelec, Dražen and Duncan I. Simester (2001), "Always Leave Home Without It. A Further Investigation of the Credit-Card Effect on Willingness to Pay," *Marketing Letters*, 12 (1), 5–12.

Puccinelli, Nancy M., Rajesh Chandrashekaran, Dhruv Grewal, and Rajneesh Suri (2013), "Are Men Seduced by Red? The Effect of Red Versus Black Prices on Price Perceptions," *Journal of Retailing*, 89 (2), 115–125.

Quattrone, George A., Cheryl P. Lawrence, Steven E. Finkel, and D. C. Andrus (1984), "Explorations in Anchoring. The Effects of Prior Range, Anchor Extremity, and Suggestive Hints," *Unpublished manuscript, Stanford University*.

Raghubir, Priya and Kirti S. Celly (2011), "Promoting Promotions. Does Showcasing Free Gifts Backfire?" *Journal of Business Research*, 64 (1), 55–58.

Raghubir, Priya and Joydeep Srivastava (2002), "Effect of Face Value on Product Valuation in Foreign Currencies," *Journal of Consumer Research*, 29 (3), 335–347.

——— (2008), "Monopoly Money. The Effect of Payment Coupling and Form on Spending Behavior," *Journal of Experimental Psychology*, 14 (3), 213–225.

——— (2009), "The Denomination Effect," *Journal of Consumer Research*, 36 (4), 701–713.

Rao, Akshay R. and Kent B. Monroe (1989), "The Effect of Price, Brand Name, and Store Name on Buyers' Perceptions of Product Quality. An Integrative Review," *Journal of Marketing Research*, 26 (3), 351–357.

Restle, Frank (1970), "Speed of Adding and Comparing Numbers," *Journal of Experimental Psychology*, 83 (2, Pt.1), 274–278.

Riener, Gerhard and Christian Traxler (2012), "Norms, Moods, and Free Lunch. Longitudinal Evidence on Payments from a Pay-What-You-Want Restaurant," *Journal of Socio-Economics*, 41 (4), 476–483.

Roth, Stefan, Lena Himbert, and Stephan Zielke (2017), "Does Unit Pricing Influence Store Price Image Dimensions and Shopping Intentions for Retail Stores?" *European Journal of Marketing*, 51 (7/8), 1396–1413.

Sagi, Adi and Nehemia Friedland (2007), "The Cost of Richness: The Effect of the Size and Diversity of Decision Sets on Post-Decision

Regret," *Journal of Personality and Social Psychology*, 93 (4), 515–524.

Sapir, Edward (1929), "A Study in Phonetic Symbolism," *Journal of Experimental Psychology*, 12 (3), 225–239.

Schindler, Robert M. (1991), "Symbolic Meanings of a Price Ending," *Advances in Consumer Research*, 18 (1), 794–801.

——— (2006), "The 99 Price Ending as a Signal of a Low-Price Appeal," *Consumer Behavior and Retailing*, 82 (1), 71–77.

Schindler, Robert M. and Thomas M. Kibarian (1996), "Increased Consumer Sales Response Through Use of 99-Ending Prices," *Consumer Behavior and Retailing*, 72 (2), 187–199.

——— (2001), "Image Communicated by the Use of 99 Endings in Advertised Prices," *Journal of Advertising*, 30 (4), 95–99.

Schindler, Robert M. and Patrick N. Kirby (1997), "Patterns of Rightmost Digits Used in Advertised Prices. Implications for Nine-Ending Effects," *Journal of Consumer Research*, 24 (2), 192–201.

Scitovszky, Tibor (1944), "Some Consequences of the Habit of Judging Quality by Price," *The Review of Economic Studies*, 12 (2), 100–105.

Shafir, Eldar, Peter Diamond, and Amos Tversky (1997), "Money Illusion," *The Quarterly Journal of Economics*, 112 (2), 341–374.

Shampanier, Kristina, Nina Mazar, and Dan Ariely (2007), "Zero as a Special Price. The True Value of Free Products," *Marketing Science*, 26 (6), 742–757.

Sharma, Dinkar and Frank P. McKenna (1998), "Differential Components of the Manual and Vocal Stroop Tasks," *Memory & Cognition*, 26 (5), 1033–1040.

Sheng, Shibin, Yeqing Bao, and Yue Pan (2007), "Partitioning or Bundling? Perceived Fairness of the Surcharge Makes a Difference," *Psychology & Marketing*, 24 (12), 1025–1041.

Sherif, Muzafer and Carl I. Hovland (1961), *Social Judgment. Assimilation and Contrast Effects in Communication and Attitude Change. Yale Studies in attitude and communication*, Vol. 4. New Haven, Conn.: Yale Univ. Press.

Sherif, Muzafer, Daniel Taub, and Carl I. Hovland (1958), "Assimilation and Contrast Effects of Anchoring Stimuli on Judgments," *Journal of Experimental Psychology*, 55 (2), 150–155.

Shiv, Baba, Ziv Carmon, and Dan Ariely (2005), "Placebo Effects of Marketing Actions: Consumers May Get What They Pay for," *Journal of Marketing Research*, 42 (4), 383–393.

Simmons, Lee C. and Robert M. Schindler (2003), "Cultural Superstitions and the Price Endings Used in Chinese Advertising," *Journal of International Marketing*, 11 (2), 101–111.

Simon, Hermann (2015), *Confessions of the Pricing Man. How Price Affects Everything*. Cham: Copernicus Books a brand of Springer.

Simonson, Itamar (1989), "Choice Based on Reasons: The Case of Attraction and Compromise Effects," *Journal of Consumer Research*, 16 (2), 158–174.

Simonson, Itamar and Amos Tversky (1992), "Choice in Context: Tradeoff Contrast and Extremeness Aversion," *Journal of Marketing Research*, 29 (3), 281–295.

Skouras, Thanos, George J. Avlonitis, and Kostis A. Indounas (2005), "Economics and Marketing on Pricing. How and Why Do They Differ?" *Journal of Product and Brand Management*, 14 (6), 362–374.

Soman, Dilip (2003), "The Effect of Payment Transparency on Consumption. Quasi-Experiments from the Field," *Marketing Letters*, 14 (3), 173–183.

Soman, Dilip and John T. Gourville (2001), "Transaction Decoupling. How Price Bundling Affects the Decision to Consume," *Journal of Marketing Research*, 38 (1), 30–44.

Somervuori, Outi (2014), "Profiling Behavioral Pricing Research in Marketing," *Journal of Product and Brand Management*, 23 (6), 462–474.

Soster, Robin L., Andrew D. Gershoff, and William O. Bearden (2014), "The Bottom Dollar Effect: The Influence of Spending to Zero on Pain of Payment and Satisfaction," *Journal of Consumer Research*, 41 (3), 656–677.

Spann, Martin and Gerard J. Tellis (2006), "Does the Internet Promote Better Consumer Decisions? The Case of Name-Your-Own-Price Auctions," *Journal of Marketing*, 70 (1), 65–78.

Stangl, Brigitte, Margit Kastner, and Girish Prayag (2017), "Pay-What-You-Want for High-Value Priced Services. Differences Between Potential, New, and Repeat Customers," *Journal of Business Research*, 74, 168–174.

Stiving, Mark and Russell S. Winer (1997), "An Empirical Analysis of Price Endings with Scanner Data," *Journal of Consumer Research*, 24 (1), 57–67.

Stock, Axel and Subramanian Balachander (2005), "The Making of a "Hot Product". A Signaling Explanation of Marketers' Scarcity Strategy," *Management Science*, 51 (8), 1181–1192.

Stoetzel, Jean, Jacques Sauerwein, and Alain de Vulpian (1954), "Reflections: French Research: Consumer Studies," in *La Psychologie Économique*, P. L. Reynaud, ed. Paris: Rivière, 183–188.

Stremersch, Stefan and Gerard J. Tellis (2002), "Strategic Bundling of Products and Prices. A New Synthesis for Marketing," *Journal of Marketing*, 66 (1), 55–72.

Suckale, Jakob and Michele Solimena (2008), "Pancreas Islets in Metabolic Signaling - Focus on the Beta-Cell," *Frontiers in Bioscience*, 13, 7156-71.

Suk, Kwanho, Jiheon Lee, and Donald R. Lichtenstein (2012), "The Influence of Price Presentation Order on Consumer Choice," *Journal of Marketing Research*, 49 (5), 708–717.

Suri, Rajneesh, Jane Z. Cai, Kent B. Monroe, and Mrugank V. Thakor (2012), "Retailers' Merchandise Organization and Price Perceptions," *Consumer Behavior and Retailing*, 88 (1), 168–179.

Suri, Rajneesh, Chiranjeev Kohli, and Kent B. Monroe (2007), "The Effects of Perceived Scarcity on Consumers' Processing of Price Information," *Journal of the Academy of Marketing Science*, 35 (1), 89–100.

Suri, Rajneesh and Kent B. Monroe (2003), "The Effects of Time Constraints on Consumers' Judgments of Prices and Products," *Journal of Consumer Research*, 30 (1), 92–104.

Suwelack, Thomas, Jens Hogreve, and Wayne D. Hoyer (2011), "Understanding Money-Back Guarantees. Cognitive, Affective, and Behavioral Outcomes," *Consumer Behavior and Retailing*, 87 (4), 462–478.

Thaler, Richard H. (1980), "Toward a Positive Theory of Consumer Choice," *Journal of Economic Behavior & Organization*, 1 (1), 39–60.

——— (1985), "Mental Accounting and Consumer Choice," *Marketing Science*, 4 (3), 199.

——— (1999), "Mental Accounting Matters," *Journal of Behavioral Decision Making*, 12 (3), 183–206.

Thaler, Richard H. and Eric J. Johnson (1990), "Gambling with the House Money and Trying to Break Even. The Effects of Prior Outcomes on Risky Choice," *Management Science*, 36 (6), 643–660.

The Telegraph (2017), "The 20 Biggest Rivalries in World Football Ranked," (accessed January 29th, 2018), [available at http://www.telegraph.co.uk/sport/football/picturegalleries/11484651/The-20-biggest-rivalries-in-world-football-ranked.html?frame=3239108].

Thomas, Manoj and Vicki G. Morwitz (2005), "Penny Wise and
    Pound Foolish: The Left-Digit Effect in Price Cognition," *Journal of
    Consumer Research*, 32 (1), 54–64.

—— (2009), "The Ease-of-Computation Effect: The Interplay of
    Metacognitive Experiences and Naive Theories in Judgments of
    Price Differences," *Journal of Marketing Research*, 46 (1), 81–91.

Thomas, Manoj, Daniel H. Simon, and Vrinda Kadiyali (2010), "The
    Price Precision Effect: Evidence from Laboratory and Market
    Data," *Marketing Science*, 29 (1), 175–190.

Tsiros, Michael and David M. Hardesty (2010), "Ending a Price Pro-
    motion: Retracting It in One Step or Phasing It Out Gradually,"
    Journal of Marketing, 74 (1), 49–64.

Tversky, Amos (1972), "Elimination by Aspects. A Theory of
    Choice," *Psychological Review*, 79 (4), 281–299.

Tversky, Amos and Daniel Kahneman (1974), "Judgment Under Un-
    certainty. Heuristics and Biases," *Science*, 185 (4157), 1124.

—— (1981), "The Framing of Decisions and the Psychology of
    Choice," *Science*, 211 (4481), 453.

—— (1991), "Loss Aversion in Riskless Choice. A Reference-De-
    pendence Model," *Quarterly Journal of Economics*, 106 (4), 1039–
    1061.

Tzelgov, Joseph, Joachim Meyer, and Avishai Henik (1992), "Auto-
    matic and Intentional Processing of Numerical Information," *Jour-
    nal of Experimental Psychology*, 18 (1), 166–179.

Urbany, Joel E., William O. Bearden, and Dan C. Weilbaker (1988),
    "The Effect of Plausible and Exaggerated Reference Prices on Con-
    sumer Perceptions and Price Search," *Journal of Consumer Re-
    search*, 15 (1), 95–110.

Vanhuele, Marc, Gilles Laurent, and Xavier Drèze (2006), "Consum-
    ers' Immediate Memory for Prices," *Journal of Consumer Research*,
    33 (2), 163–172.

Veblen, Thorstein (1899), *The Theory of the Leisure Class. An Eco-
    nomic Study of Institutions*. New York: Macmillan.

Verhallen, Theo M.M. and Henry S.J. Robben (1994), "Scarcity and
    Preference. An Experiment on Unavailability and Product Evalua-
    tion," *Journal of Economic Psychology*, 15 (2), 315–331.

Völckner, Franziska and Julian Hofmann (2007), "The Price-Per-
    ceived Quality Relationship. A Meta-Analytic Review and Assess-
    ment of Its Determinants," *Marketing Letters*, 18 (3), 181–196.

Waber, Rebecca L., Baba Shiv, Ziv Carmon, and Dan Ariely (2008),
    "Commercial Features of Placebo and Therapeutic Efficacy," *Jour-
    nal of the American Medical Association*, 299 (9), 1016–1017.

Wadhwa, Monica and Kuangjie Zhang (2015), "This Number Just Feels Right: The Impact of Roundedness of Price Numbers on Product Evaluations," *Journal of Consumer Research*, 41 (5), 1172–1185.

Wang, Tong V., Rogier J.D. Potter van Loon, Martijn J. van den Assem, and Dennie van Dolder (2016), "Number Preferences in Lotteries," *Judgment and Decision Making*, 11 (3), 243–259.

Wansink, Brian, Robert J. Kent, and Stephen J. Hoch (1998), "An Anchoring and Adjustment Model of Purchase Quantity Decisions," *Journal of Marketing Research*, 35 (1), 71–81.

Wathieu, Luc, A. V. Muthukrishnan, and Bart J. Bronnenberg (2004), "The Asymmetric Effect of Discount Retraction on Subsequent Choice," *Journal of Consumer Research*, 31 (3), 652–657.

Wertenbroch, Klaus, Dilip Soman, and Amitava Chattopadhyay (2007), "On the Perceived Value of Money. The Reference Dependence of Currency Numerosity Effects," *Journal of Consumer Research*, 34 (1), 1–10.

Westjohn, Stanford A., Holger Roschk, and Peter Magnusson (2017), "Eastern Versus Western Culture Pricing Strategy. Superstition, Lucky Numbers, and Localization," *Journal of International Marketing*, 25 (1), 72–90.

Wilson, Timothy D., Christopher E. Houston, Kathryn M. Etling, and Nancy Brekke (1996), "A New Look at Anchoring Effects. Basic Anchoring and Its Antecedents," *Journal of Experimental Psychology*, 125 (4), 387–402.

Winer, Russell S. (2005), *Pricing. Relevant knowledge series.* Cambridge, Mass: Marketing Science Inst.

Xia, Lan (2003), "Consumers' Judgments of Numerical and Price Information," *Journal of Product and Brand Management*, 12 (5), 275–292.

Xia, Lan and Kent B. Monroe (2004), "Price Partitioning on the Internet," *Journal of Interactive Marketing*, 18 (4), 63–73.

Xia, Lan, Kent B. Monroe, and Jennifer L. Cox (2004), "The Price Is Unfair! A Conceptual Framework of Price Fairness Perceptions," *Journal of Marketing*, 68 (4), 1–15.

Yadav, Manjit S. (1994), "How Buyers Evaluate Product Bundles. A Model of Anchoring and Adjustment," *Journal of Consumer Research*, 21 (2), 342–353.

——— (1995), "Bundle Evaluation in Different Market Segments. The Effects of Discount Framing and Buyers' Preference Heterogeneity," *Journal of the Academy of Marketing Science*, 23 (3), 206.

Yang, Sybil S., Sheryl E. Kimes, and Mauro M. Sessarego (2009), "Menu Price Presentation Influences on Consumer Purchase Behavior in Restaurants," *International Journal of Hospitality Management*, 28 (1), 157–160.

Yi, Youjae (1990), "The Effects of Contextual Priming in Print Advertisements," *Journal of Consumer Research*, 17 (2), 215–222.

Bonus Updates

As research is always evolving, I regularly create updates to this book. These updates follow the same structure as this book and seamlessly integrate into the presented structure of psychological pricing effects.

You find these exclusive updates in the Readers Area on the accompanying website:

Link: *www.PsychologyOfPricing.com/readersarea*
Password: freeforreaders

If you are looking for sparks of inspirations on an ongoing basis, I invite to check out my newsletter on *Pricing Nuggets*. These nuggets are brief insights carved out of lengthy academic papers. The library of past nuggets is available here:

Link: *www.PsychologyOfPricing.com/nuggets*

Made in the USA
Middletown, DE
27 February 2021

34503485R00106